STUDIES IN

Sanskrit Dramatic Criticism

"Ananyādhīnakalyāṇān bhaktamaṅgalasādhakān
Yogīndrān sadgurūn vande Śrī-nṛsiṁha-sarasvatīn".

T.G. Mainkar M.A., Ph.D., D. Litt.
R.G. Bhandarkar Professor of Sanskrit, Bombay University.
Ex-Principal, Fergusson College, Poona. Dean, Faculty
of Arts, University of Poona. Professor of
Sanskrit, Delhi University.

MOTILAL BANARSIDASS
DELHI :: PATNA :: VARANASI

Head Office : BUNGALOW ROAD, JAWAHAR NAGAR, DELHI-7
Branches : (1) CHOWK, VARANASI-1 (U.P.)
(2) ASHOK RAJPATH, PATNA-4 (BIHAR)

First Edition
1971

Printed in India

BY SHANTILAL JAIN AT SHRI JAINENDRA PRESS, BUNGALOW ROAD, JAWAHAR NAGAR, DELHI-7 AND PUBLISHED BY SUNDARLAL JAIN, MOTILAL BANARSIDASS, BUNGALOW ROAD, JAWAHAR NAGAR, DELHI-7.

To
My Teacher
Professor R.S. Joag
with profound gratefulness.

PREFACE

Commentaries on the various Sanskrit plays fascinated me very much when I went through them while working on the problem of the Sandhis and the Sandhyaṅgas in the Nāṭya-śāstra of Bharata. This dissertation is an outcome of that fascination.

Like the dramatists themselves, the commentators too are very colourful personalities and it is a sheer joy to read their improvements over the lines from the recognised masters of Sanskrit poetry, their explanations and suggestions, their exposition of Dhvani and their erudite discussions of the figures of speech as well as those of other dramaturgic details. Like their modern counterparts they also try to interpret and read allegories and are capable of pleasant as well as fierce irony.

It is an unfortunate trend to neglect these commentaries. Often very sweeping generalizations, based primarily on ignorance and perhaps through a prejudice towards Sanskrit and hard work, are made condemning these commentaries as 'useless literature'. A serious student of Sanskrit, however, cannot afford to neglect this precious treasure. I will feel amply rewarded if his interest in the commentaries is awakened and he feels an urge to peruse them.

I am very much grateful to Messrs Motilal Banarsidass who have always taken very keen interest in my work and have taken considerable troubles to carry out the printing of the book as faultlessly as possible. They have been all kindness and courtesy throughout. My best thanks are due to them. Similarly, my best thanks are due to Dr. (Miss) Usha R. Bhise, my colleague in the Department who spared no pains while correcting the proofs.

T.G. Mainkar

CONTENTS

I. INTRODUCTORY

Every serious student of Sanskrit Drama is very familiar with the names of Rāghavabhaṭṭa, Jagaddhara, Pūrṇasarasvatī Tripurāri, Ghanaśyāma, Ḍhunḍhirāja, Kāṭayavema, Vīrarāghava Abhirāma, Śivarāma, for these worthies have enabled him to appreciate many beautiful and significant places in the dramas on which they have commented, places the full significance of which he could not have so easily understood. The contribution that these commentators make to our appreciation of the Sanskrit dramas is really very significant and it would be no exaggeration to say that some of these commentaries can indeed be regarded as very brilliant pieces of literary criticism.

When one thinks of Sanskrit dramaturgy and Sanskrit dramas, one cannot afford in any manner to neglect these Sanskrit commentators. If the writers on Sanskrit dramaturgy present to us the theory of Sanskrit drama and if the dramatists give us the works of dramatic art, it is these commentators who apply the canons of dramaturgy to these plays. They try to analyse and understand the play in the light of the doctrines and views of the writers on dramaturgy. They, therefore, form a very vital link between the writers on dramaturgy on the one hand and the dramatists on the other, for it is they who give us the application of the theory of the former as applied to the works of the latter. One can in this context refer to the detailed discussions regarding the Nāndī, its different forms and its significance in the play, the different Sandhis and the various Sandhyaṅgas used in the play and so also about the Nāṭyabhūṣaṇas and the Nāṭya-alaṅkāras used in the different plays that one gets in all these commentaries. A point of interest and of great importance that deserves to be noticed is that while pointing out these different elements in the drama, they have given the definitions of the Aṅgas, the Nāṭyabhūṣaṇas, the Bhāvas, and the Alaṅkāras, so they furnish indirectly very valuable evidence for a reconstruction of a critical edition of the works they quote from. A text like that of Bharata's Nāṭyaśāstra is known to be corrupt and when a definition that is at variance with that of Bharata is seen as given by these commentators, then it does mean a valuable help for not only a proper understanding of the text of Bharata, but also help for a correct understanding of the doctrine that Bharata seeks to teach. The same is true for the other texts from which they quote.

In this connection a point deserves some special emphasis. These commentators, as has been observed, apply the doctrines of dramaturgy to the plays and in doing so, naturally indicate where a particular element, say a Sandhyaṅga or a Bhāva or a Nāṭyabhūṣaṇa is to be seen as used. Students of Bharata know very well that he always defines but does not illustrate at all. Other writers like Dhanañjaya, Rāmacandra, Guṇacandra, Sāgaranandin and others who followed Bharata in the field of dramaturgy also define and illustrate as well, but their illustrations more than often, are drawn from the plays like the Ratnāvali and the Veṇīsaṁhāra though a few like Rāmacandra are seen to cast their net wide. What the author of the Nāṭyaśāstra had in mind is to be understood, first in the light of the explanation offered by Abhinavagupta and then in the light of the definitions and the illustrations furnished by these successors of Bharata. The commentators on Sanskrit plays, therefore, are to be regarded as making a really valuable contribution to a proper understanding of the original ideas of Bharata when they give us illustrations from the plays like the Abhijñānaśākuntala, the Uttararāmacarita, the Mudrārākṣasa, the Mālatīmādhava and the Mālavikāgnimitra. Many of the Sandhyaṅgas, Bhūṣaṇas and Alaṅkāras which appear as riddles and somewhat enigmatic, become clear when understood with this additional help from these commentators. The reflections of the controversies as well as the divergent views regarding the different dramaturgic concepts are to be seen in these commentaries also, for we see some commentators, for instance in the matter of the Sandhis and their Aṅgas following the view that a particular Sandhyaṅga belongs to a particular Sandhi only or a Sandhyaṅga is to be used only once while there are others like Jagaddhara who do not subscribe to this view and hold that there is no such restriction and that a Sandhyaṅga could be used anywhere and repeatedly too. These commentators point out the Arthaprakṛtis, the Avasthās, the Sandhis and the Sandhyaṅgas but all of them curiously enough appear to follow the Bharata tradition. What is meant by this assertion is that in Abhinavagupta and in Śāradātanaya we find references to divergent views regarding the Avasthās, the Sandhis and even as regards their nomenclatures also, but none of the commentators is seen either following these other views or even referring to them. In a sense this is understandable, for Abhinavagupta and Śāradātanaya refer to the views that were held in the preceding eras, while most of the commentators belong to an era that was separated from them by many centuries and in the meanwhile only the Bharata tradition had remained alive. The various traditions mentioned by Abhinavagupta and also the traditions of Harṣa and Subandhu which Śāradātanaya is seen mentioning, appear to have fallen in the background and neglected. These commentaries, in this manner, are important from the point of view of a critical reconstruction of a text, for a proper understanding of the dramaturgic doctrines and concepts and also from the point of view of history of dramaturgy in general. There cannot be any doubt about the fact that for a historian of Sanskrit Dramaturgy these commentaries are sources invaluable.

These commentators in their commentaries reveal their familiarity with the Sanskrit classical literature and with other branches of Sanskrit learning too, just as they display their thorough grasp of dramaturgy. They quote from several works and authors and in this respect their reading appears to be very wide indeed. They often quote from other dramatists and poets to draw our attention to parallels. One may in this context refer to the commentaries of Pūrṇasarasvatī, Ghanaśyāma, and Sundarī and Kamalā. A very natural result of this practice of the commentators is that we come to know many authors and their works. For instance, we find Ghanaśyāma, in his commentary, the Sañjīvana, on the

Uttararāmacarita refers to the following authors: Vālmīki, Bhartṛmīḍha, Śrīnātha, Hāsamiśra, Vikramārka, Jayadeva, Daṇḍin, Bodhāyana, Bhaṭṭi, Kālidāsa, Murāri, Bhartṛhari, Māgha, Īśvarakṛṣṇamiśra, Līlādhara, Gauḍapāda, Varadanta, Prabhākaramiśra and Bāṇa. The list of works to which he refers is equally impressive. The Kośas from which he quotes are simply numerous and some of these Kośas are no longer extant. Kapila, Kedāra, Agastya, Māṭhara, Nandi, Saṁsārāvarta are mere names to us. Viewed in this light, it will be very easily seen what a fund of valuable information about Sanskrit works and authors these commentaries supply. They can be expected to enable us to fill in the gaps in our knowledge of the Sanskrit literature as a whole. To a historian of Sanskrit literature, therefore, these commentaries should prove to be a good source of information.

If these commentaries are thus very useful for a study of Sanskrit dramaturgy and literature, their importance for a study of another branch of knowledge, closely allied to dramaturgy, that of Poetics, is also equally great. These commentators usually take care to point out the Alaṅkāras, quoting the relevant definitions everytime and discuss them when they feel it necessary to do so. They point out the elements that contribute to the excellence of the composition and often they write at length to make certain ideas absolutely clear. To illustrate this point one can refer to the comments of Rāghavabhaṭṭa on the celebrated verse II. 1. in his Arthadyotanikā on the Abhijñānaśākuntala. The verse runs:

"Kāmam priyā na sulabhā manastu tadbhāvadarśanāśvāsi /
akṛtārthe'pi manasije ratimubhayaprārthanā kurute //"
(AS.II.1)

Rāghavabhaṭṭa comments: "Sā kāmam atyartham priyā priyatamā ityarthaḥ / tarhi samyageva / na samyagityāha-yato na sulabhā prāpyā kintu sukhena na labhyā / tarhi duṣprāpe vastuni prayatnenāpi kimityāśaṅkāyām āha-mana iti / tu iti śaṅkocchede/ manas tasyā nāyikāyā bhavaś ceṣṭās tāsām darśanāyāsi / sakhedam prayatnapūrvakam ālasmītyarthaḥ / akṛteti / manasije 'kṛtārthe'pyubhayaprārthanā svasyābhilāṣo ratim rāgam kurute prītim utpādayati / jātaratyoḥ sambhavatītyarthaḥ/ atrākṛtārthe' pyajātaratyāderapītyapiśabdārthaḥ / tenaitaduktam bhavati / yathā manmanasastadbhāvadarśanalālasatvam kāryam samarthyate tenārthāntaranyāsaḥ / Uktam ca rājānakarucakena-sāmānyaviśeṣakāryakāraṇabhāvābhyām nirdiṣṭam prakṛtasamarthanam arthāntaranyāsaḥ-' iti / sa ca hi-śabdopadānupādānābhyām dvidhā iti uktaḥ / atra ca hi-śabdānupādāne boddhavyaḥ / Udbhaṭādimate sāmānyaviśeṣabhāva evārthāntaranyāsāṅgīkārād atra kāvyaliṅgameva / yeṣām mate kāryakāraṇabhāve arthāntaranyāsaḥ teṣām mata etat-vyatiriktaviṣayatvam kāvyaliṅgasya ity avadheyam / atha ca manasijaḥ kandarpaḥ akṛtārthaḥ / ratiḥ kāmabhāryā ca iti virodhaḥ / vyākhyātaprītiparyāyatvena virodhābhāsaḥ / 'ratiḥ kāmastriyām rāge surate'pi ratiḥ smṛtā'iti dharaṇīḥ / Śrutyanuprāsaśca / anena pūrvānurāgavipralambhād abhilāṣo nāmāvasthā uktā / tallakṣaṇam tu sudhākare-'saṅgamopāyaracitā prārabdhādhyavasāyataḥ / saṅkalpecchāsamudbhūtiḥ abhilāṣā itīritaḥ' iti /" (p. 43)

The passage has been given in full deliberately only with a view to showing how Rāghavabhaṭṭa writes almost an essay on the alaṅkāra in this apparently very simple verse from Kālidāsa. After having explained the verse, word by word and having made the sense perfectly clear he proceeds to discuss the alaṅkāra and first discusses the presence of the Arthāntaranyāsa, then of the Kāvyaliṅga, and lastly, of the Virodhābhāsa. In his analysis he has referred to Rājānaka Rucaka and Udbhaṭa and given us their views. His own contribution appears to be the pointing out of the alaṅkāra Virodhābhāsa, since he has supported it by a quotation from the Kośa Dharaṇi about the meaning of the word 'rati'. He has not failed to notice the presence of the 'Śrutyanuprāsa' in the verse and finally has linked the verse with the delineation of the character and with the 'rasa' in the play by pointing out that this verse represents the 'avasthā', the stage known as 'abhilāṣa' in the mind of Duṣyanta; the stage 'cintā' having been already shown and referred to in the words of the Vidūṣaka, earlier. These remarks enable us to understand the gradual rise and development as well as the intensity of the feeling of love in the hero which urges him to proceed further in the matter as he does. Rāghavabhaṭṭa has, it can be said, done remarkably well in bringing out the full significance of the verse in discussing the Alaṅkāras in the verse and finally in placing it in its proper place in the general development of the play and in the development of the emotion in the hero, the speaker of the verse. After reading these comments of Rāghavabhaṭṭa one comes to notice the very deceptive simplicity of Kālidāsian pieces as well as the possibility of missing so much of importance and interest in them. We also find Rāghavabhaṭṭa and other commentators too, discussing the metres, their schemes and the use of a particular metre in a particular context and its contribution to the 'rasa' in the play.

If the present discussion of Rāghavabhaṭṭa shows how the Alaṅkāra aspects were carefully attended to by the commentators, one can refer to the comments of Tripurāri on I.20 in the Mālatīmādhava, to show that they were equally careful and interested in discussing the 'rasa' aspects both in the verses and in the play as a whole. The verse in question runs:

> "Gamanamalasaṁ, śūnyā dṛṣṭiḥ, śarīram asauṣṭhavaṁ
> śvasitam adhikaṁ kiṁvetat syāt kimanyad ato'thavā /
> bhramati bhuvane kandarpājñā, vikāri ca yauvanaṁ
> lalitamadhurās te te bhāvāḥ kṣipanti ca dhīratām //"
> (MM.I.20)

Tripurāri very meticulously points out as to how the different Vyabhicāribhāvas like 'ālasya, cintā, glāni, śrama, viṣāda, moha and the Avasthā 'anusmṛti' have been skilfully used by the poet to delineate the 'vipralambha'. The Alaṅkāra has been declared to be sasandehā' niścayāntasamuccayālaṇkāra. It has also been pointed out that the temple of Cupid and the adjacent garden, the 'madanodyāna' are to be looked upon as the 'uddīpana vibhāvas' of this 'śṛṅgāra'. In his discussion he has also taken troubles to define 'ālasya, glāni, yauvana and dhairya' and has once quoted from Bhāvaprakāśa. (pp. 20, 21). Tripurāri has really done well in laying before us the full significance of the details given to us by Bhavabhūti about his hero Mādhava here. Such discussions should prove the importance of these commentaries from the point of view of studies in Poetics. In this respect, these commentaries can be regarded as interesting complimentary works to the regular works on rhetorics where these different elements, though defined and illustrated fail to make impression on us being given in a a piecemeal fashion. It is in these commentaries that we get the full scheme applied to a work of literary art and also analysed with the necessary explanations. It is impossible to exaggerate their importance from this point of view.

It has been already observed that these commentators often refer to the different lexicons in Sanskrit literature and quote from them to support their points. This practice of the commentators naturally throws a flood of light on the lexicographical literature that was once available to a student of Sanskrit. Amara, Haima, Medinī, Dharaṇi, Viśva, Vaijayantī, Śāśvata, Yādava, Halāyudha, Akṣaya are the usual ones often referred to, but we also come to know of the Kośas which are mentioned as Agastya, Dvirūpa, Kedāra, Saṁsārāvarta, Māṭhara, Nandī and others which today are nothing more than names to us. Ghanaśyāma takes particular pride in describing himself as a 'Kośāvalivallabha' and one feels inclined to concede his point when one considers the number of Kośas that he has referred to in his commentaries. From this point of history and knowledge of rich lexicographical literature in Sanskrit, the value of these commentaries is immense.

Most of these commentators are very sound grammarians and usually quote from the authorities on Grammar often giving the relevant Sūtras. Ghanaśyāma is seen quoting even from Prākrit Grammarians Vararuci and Hemacandra in support of his contentions and thus considered, these commentaries on account of these grammatical discussions are helpful for our studies from the point of view of Grammar also. When these commentators discuss words, they explain it and also point out its 'Deśī' character if the word happens to be so, and also many times take care to give the provincial equivalent. Such matter, which is available in these commentaries is useful for our study of the languages concerned. The commentators often enter into discussions of Prākrit dialects like the Śaurasenī, Māgadhī and the like and many times point out the mistakes of the playwrights. One may refer in this context to the commentaries of Ghanaśyāma and also to that of Sundarī and Kamalā. From a linguistic point of view also, therefore, a study of these commentaries is bound to yield its reward.

These commentators are learned scholars and some of them are poets as well. In the opening and concluding verses of their commentaries, they invariably give an account of themselves and also an idea of their attainments. Ghanaśyāma informs us that he was a great poet, 'kavīnām kaviḥ, and a 'Kośāvali-vallabha'. Jagaddhara tells us that he was a well-read man especially in the Nyāya of Gotama, the Kośas and the Kāvyas, the Grammar of Pāṇini 'Pāṇinīyam matam', Chandas and Alaṅkāra-śāstra and in Bharata. Rāghavabhaṭṭa, Ḍhuṇḍhirāja and others too reveal in ample measure their knowledge of the different branches of Sanskrit learning and it could be said that they took special care to prepare themselves with all the necessary intellectual attainments and a knowledge of the disciplines, before they chose to put on the mantle of a critic. They knew the responsibility involved and, therefore, undertook the task only after properly equipping themselves. They were aware of the fact that they had a double duty to perform: to point out the excellences of literary art before them and also to enable a lover of literature, a 'sahṛdaya', to understand and appreciate the same. To do justice to the artist and to help the reader also, was their double aim and there should be no difficulty, after a careful study of their commentaries, in readily conceding that they have discharged the duties expected of a critic in a very remarkable manner.

They had the necessary sympathy and reverence for the artists whose works they sought to explain, but at the same time they had their own independent views and whenever they felt it necessary, they have not at all hesitated to point out what they considered as mistakes and flaws even in the works of great poets Kālidāsa and Bhavabhūti. In this context one can refer to the commentary of Ghanaśyāma on the Uttararāmacarita where both Bhavabhūti, its author and Kālidāsa have come in for criticism at his hands. Thus, in the First Act when Sītā asks Lakṣmaṇa about Ūrmilā in 'iyam aparā kā' Lakṣmaṇa's reply is given as 'salajjasmitam / apavārya'. Ghanaśyāma points out that this cannot be 'apavārya' since 'apavārya' is a talk with some character other than the one who puts the question and this is not the case here. He adds ironically that it could be said in defence that Lakṣmaṇa here is talking with his own mind. Ghanaśyāma observes:

> 'Raho'nyena sahoktau syād apavārya janāntikam' iti lakṣaṇāt prakṛte anyena samādheyam / saha bhāṣaṇābhāvat kaveḥ pramādaḥ / athāpi 'svamanasā saha'iti dayayā /

Here is another place. Towards the close of the first Act Lakṣmaṇa asks Sītā to mount the chariot. Bhavabhūti makes Sītā say'iam āruhāmi / (utthāya parikramya) phurai me gabbhabhāro, saniam gacchāhma'. Ghanaśyāma thinks that as far as he sees it, no lady would refer, without any shyness, so openly to her advanced state of pregnancy and therefore the poet is wrong here. Considerations of propriety, therefore, would require a better arrangement of this speech and he would suggest that 'phurai me gabbhabhāro' should be a 'svagata' and 'prakāśam' would be 'saniam gacchāmha'. His words are: "Ittham puruṣasamakṣaṁ niḥsaṅkocatayā kathanam kaveḥ acāturyam / asmākam tu nirbhāti-svagatam-phurai me gabbhabhāro / prakāśam-saniam gacchāmo / iti pāṭhakramaḥ tāvad atra viśeṣajñāḥ pramāṇam iti". (p.30)

One may refer to yet another interesting place. In the third Act Vāsantī refers to the 'latāgṛha'where Rāma waited for Sītā who tarried, being attracted by the swans and on entering it, folded her hands before him, 'mugdhaḥ praṇāmāñjaliḥ' as if to tender her apologies. Ghanaśyāma considers this 'act of folding hands' as shown by Bhavabhūti 'improper', for ladies from high families do not 'fold their hands' an act which is proper for the courtezans. He observes:

> "Añjalir iti kathanam kaveḥ acāturyam / veśyājanakriyamāṇaḥ ayam vilāsaḥ na tu kulāṅganānāṁ sampradāyaḥ / kadācit aparādhe sati satyāḥ pādapīḍanam eva āracayantītaram, ity uccaisśirasaḥ / alaukikavaidikaghaṇṭāpāṭhamanthaviśeṣajñaḥ pramāṇam" / (p.74)

One may or may not agree with the commentator in all that he has to say at these places, but it would be clearly seen that he does not hesitate to say what he honestly feels and that he is not daunted by any name, howsoever great. Thus both Kālidāsa and Bhavabhūti, who have used the form 'dīrye' in 'na vidīrye kaṭhināḥ khalu striyaḥ' and in' dīrye kiṁ na sahasradhāhamathavā rāmeṇa kim duṣkaram' respectively have been censured by Ghanaśyāma by observing 'kaveḥ pramādaḥ dayanīyaḥ'. This is a very healthy and an absolute necessity in literary criticism worth the name.

But this does not mean that these commentators have no respect for the playwrights. They realize the greatness of the authors, for thus does Rāghavabhaṭṭa comment on the word 'Kālidāsa' in the Abhijñānaśākuntala in the celebrated 'kālidāsa-grathita-vastunā'. (p.5).

> 'Kālidāseti kavipraśaṁsā / Jagadvilakṣaṇasya atipratītasya nāmāntareṇa sarasvatīvapuṣaḥ tasya nāmasaṅkīrtanam eva stutiḥ' /

Even Ghanaśyāma, after all his bitter criticism, does recognise that the author of the Uttararāmacarita, Bhavabhūti is a great poet, a 'mahākavi'. It would thus appear that in these commentators we have a very desirable and a rare combination of due respect and an independence of spirit.

With such scholarly minds, capable of independent thinking, a difference of opinion is to be taken for granted and we therefore need not be surprised if we find in these commentaries severe attacks on those commentators from whom they differ. These views of others are referred to in the usual manner of Sanskrit writers as 'iti kecit' or 'iti apare' or 'iti anye'. A comparative study of commentaries by different commentators on one and the same play is very interesting and instructive from this point of view. One can refer in this context, by way of an illustration to the three commentaries of Tripurāri, Jagaddhara and Pūrṇasarasvatī on the Mālatīmādhava of Bhavabhūti. These commentators differ from each other and so criticise each other. Often one comes across very brilliant expositions and to illustrate the point one can refer to these very commentaries and especially to the masterly exposition by all the three commentators of the celebrated verse of Bhavabhūti which runs as :

> 'Līneva pratibimbiteva likhitevotkīrṇarūpeva ca
> pratyupteva ca vajralepaghaṭitevāntarnikhāteva ca /
> sā naś cetasi kīliteva viśikhaiś cetobhuvaḥ pañcabhiḥ
> cintāsantatitantujālanibiḍasyūteva lagnā priyā //
>
> MM. v. 10.

Bhavabhūti is no doubt deliberately erudite here as his preceding scene serving as a preface to this verse would clearly indicate. Vīrarāghava (pp. 117-118) explains every word in this verse bringing out the significance in each case thus:

Mādhava speaks of himself as 'naḥ' in plural for it indicates his own 'greatness, luck and importance' in that Mālatī had fallen in love with him—mayi anuraktā āsaktacittā iti aho me saubhāgyam iti ātmani gauravam āropya bahuvacanam. And now she has been fixed in his mind, 'līnā' like a drop of water in a heap of dust—thus hidden in; but then she would not flash forth, hence 'pratibimbitā', reflected in my mind like the orb of the moon in a clear lake; but how could there be a reflection when the original is absent, hence 'likhitā' painted on the canvass of my mind by the God of of Love with the brush of 'thought' add colours of 'love'; but then this would only be a picture and not she herself, hence 'utkīrṇā', the sculptor Cupid has carved her out of my mind with his arrows; but then the mind is atomic and also without parts, hence 'pratyuptā', this jewel of a lady is fixed in the mind melted by the fire of separation; but then such a fixing has in it a possibility of a falling off or separation, hence 'vajralepaghaṭitā' fixed in a very firm manner with a hard and firm plaster; but then plastering would perhaps mean an absence of contact between the mind and the beloved, hence 'antarnikhātā', she was placed deep in the mind like a treasure in the ground; but then she might not be seen at all, hence 'kīlitā', she has been nailed into the mind by Cupid with his arrows; but then how could the very frail mind and the delicate dame both suffer this nailing with the arrows, so 'syūta', delicately sewn with the threads of thought. Vīrarāghava adds that the figure of speech, Alaṅkāra, here is 'Utprekṣā' and that many in their interpretation of this verse begin with 'syūta' and end with 'līna', for that way is secured an ascending order of oneness between the lover and the beloved, probably relying on the maxim that the sense must dominate over the text, 'pāṭhakramāt arthakramaḥ balīyān'. But we can also understand here a significant sequence in the description in the 'pāṭhakrama' from 'līna' to syūta' in the manner just indicated. It can be conceded that the commentator has certainly done his best in fully explaining this 'mālotprekṣā' the string of charming fancies, which he understands as 'ekasya anekadhā adhyavasāyāt ca'—on account of one being regarded in many ways.

Jagaddhara, on the other hand, understands this figure of speech as 'Upamā' since he explains as 'sarvatra atra lagnatvasya prakāra-bhedena upamā-bhedaḥ'. (pp. 62-63). This seriated expression is the result of an inner dissatisfaction felt at the earlier expression by the the lover-and of cource by the poet too—'pūrvapūrva—aparitoṣāt vā'. He explains: an entity though present may not be seen as for instance the salt in water which is 'līna, so is Mālatī in the mind of Mādhava; but this may mean that she is not seen at all, hence she is 'pratibimbitā' reflected as a red—flower in a crystal; but the reflection may imply both, a duality and distance, so she is 'likhitā' drawn like letters on a paper; but such written stuff might be soiled by water and the like, hence she is 'utkīrṇā' carved, so it conveys a permanence; but then this might mean that she is only a portion of the mind and not the whole mind, hence she is 'pratyuptā' mounted on it like a jewel on a ring and not only chiselled out of the mind but this might again mean a possibility of the loss of contact, hence she is 'vajralepaghaṭitā', firmly plastered, but this too has a smell of externality so she is 'antarnikhātā', carved within, deeply placed within, like the roots in the soil; but then the roots are also often uprooted, hence she is 'kīlitā', nailed to the mind with the five arrows of Cupid; but this also is not enough and hence 'syūta', she has been sewn with the threads of thought.

So far, Jagaddhara explains these ideas of Mālatī being firmly set in the mind of Mādhava, very much in the same manner as does Vīrarāghava, yet with his own significant illustrations, but what deserves to be noted is that he proceeds to explain further that in 'līnatvam' we have a reference to the Yogācāra view that the relation between the subject and the object, the 'viṣaya' and the 'viṣayin' is 'ātmarūpa' while in 'pratibimbita' the position stated is that of the Sāṅkhyas, according to whom it is always the Self that is reflected. The description 'likhitā' is in accordance with the Sāutrāntika view that it is knowledge that lends its shape to the object, while the Tridaṇḍi view is reflected in 'utkīrṇā' since it regards the 'caitanya' as transformed into the object. The phrase 'pratyuptā' refers to the Pātañjala view wherein a new shape is contemplated after the suppression of the former one and 'vajralepaghaṭitā' reflects the Nyāya theory which regards two independents being firmly brought together when the 'viṣaya' and the 'viṣayin' come together. In the phrase 'antarnikhātā' we have a reference to the celebrated Vijñanavāda view that things are embedded in the mind and have no external existence. These are the different views regarding the relation that exists between the 'viṣaya' and the 'viṣayin' of the different systems of philosophical thought—'viṣaya—viṣayi—bhāva—vikalpāḥ'—and Jagaddhara is perhaps here more subtle than the other commentators for he makes us regard all this as perfectly natural in the case of Mādhava who is a student of logic, Ānvīkṣikī, as Kāmandakī pointedly informs us at the outset.

But perhaps one may be tempted to regard the performance of Pūrṇasarasvatī here as the best of the three. He connects the word 'antaḥ' with each of the words, 'līnā, pratibimbitā, likhitā, utkīrṇā, pratyuptā, and vajralepaghaṭitā though it occurs only with 'nikhātā'—antaḥśabdaḥ līnevetyādibhiḥ pratyekam abhisambandhanīyaḥ. After this, he has for every idea drawn a parallel from other poets and has elucidated his own discussion with them. He observes that 'līnā' might suggest an entry into the heart either on account of fear or bashfulness, hence 'pratibimbitā', reflected. How could the figure of Mālatī enter the atomic mind? She was reflected as in a mirror. But such a reflection is likely to perish when either the mirror or the original is withdrawn, so 'likhitā', painted, which bestows permanancy. But a painting has the danger from water and similar other damaging factors, hence 'utkīrṇā' but here too the all—devouring time may have its effects hence 'pratyuptā' she has been fixed like a jewel in a piece of gold, but then this might result in a partial perception only, hence she was 'vajralepaghaṭitā' placed in the mind firmly held, like a goddess firmly placed on a footstool. But such plasterings, howsoever strong, succumb to the ravages of time hence 'antarnikhātā, she was placed deep in the mind like some rich treasure in the ground. This is thus an ascending series and what is finally conveyed is that the beloved has been so firmly placed in the mind that now she is beyond any exit, destruction, fading of beauty, any partial or incomplete view and also unsteadiness. The different 'utprekṣās are linked with each other and should not be taken separately—'pūrva—pūrvākāṅkṣānivāritayā utprekṣā—śṛṅkhalayā....atiśayitaḥ arthaḥ sahṛdaya—hṛdayahārī samarpyate. Paraspara—nirapekṣatayā vyākhyāne kaḥ camatkāraḥ. (p. 268).

This particular discussion by the three commentators on the Mālatīmādhava v. 10, has been given at some length only to show that a careful reading of all the available and different commentaries on a play is very refreshing and has its own rewards. It would be a pathetic mistake to regard these commentators as dull-witted and given mostly to a discussion of problems lexicographical and grammatical. Scholars, undoubtedly, they were, but what is of greater importance is the fact that they did have in them, in ample measure, that subtle sensitivity and poetic temperament which alone can make one a successful commentator of a classic piece of literary art. A Sanskrit commentator, therefore, is a very pleasing personality, a friend to be met with and not an erudite pedant to be shunned. When these commentators tried to comment on the plays before them, they were fully aware of their responsibilities. If some of them are seen writing in a somewhat terse manner, that has to be put down as the genius of the language in which they wrote. But even in this respect of style, commentators like Rāghavabaṭṭa, Pūrṇasarasvatī. Vīrarāghava do show that they have cultivated their own charming style.

These commentators, it is to be noted, differ and show independence of spirit, not only in the matter of interpretations of verses or a few passages in a play but they take up discussions of wider issues relevant and important and reveal independent thinking in their viewpoints. As an illustration one may refer to the discussion regarding the precise form and nature of the marriage of Mālatī and Mādhava in the Mālatīmādhava to be met with in the commentaries. Pūrṇasarasvatī is inclined to regard the marriage to be of the Prājāpatya type while Jagaddhara regards the same to be of the celebrated Gāndharva type. Arguments are made in favour of the desired type and in support help is sought from the Dharmaśāstra literature. This will only show how these commentators did not interest themselves in merely explaining or paraphrasing the original text before them but also indulged in discussions of matters in which criticism in its broad sense is expected to take a keen interest. Ghanaśyāma too, in his commentary on the Uttararāmacarita refers to his rivals and does not spare them when he holds a view different from that of theirs. A point of great importance sometimes emerges from these discussions especially when they centre round the different readings, the Pāṭhabhedas, that the commentators notice. The importance of these Pāṭhabhedas and of the conclusions of these commentators cannot be exaggerated or overstated from the point of view of textual criticism and a reconstruction of the correct text of the work they comment upon.

The importance of these commentaries is further enhanced by the fact that we have also in some of them an effort to explain a work as an allegory and one may in this context refer to the commentary of Pūrṇasarasvatī on the Mālatīmādhava. One can also mention the commentary of the disciple (whose name we do not know) of Nārāyaṇa Bhaṭṭa on the Bhagavadajjukīya Prahasana of Bodhāyana where an ingenious attempt is made to explain the farce as an allegory having a very serious import. These are commendable efforts that evoke our admiration.

At times the commentators are seen putting forth some interesting suggestions. One may or may not accept them. Sundarī and Kamalā in their commentary on the Viddhaśālabhañjikā of Rājaśekhara take pains to point out that Rājaśekhara belonged to Mahārāṣṭra. Ghanaśyāma has a curious suggestion to make while commenting on the well-known line of Bhavabhūti.

'Yam brahmāṇam iyam devī vāgvaśyevānuvartate' URC. I. 2. in the Uttararāmacarita that here the poet is jealous of Kālidāsa. He observes:

> 'brahmāṇam satkarmaniratam. anena antarmukhe' py ucchṛṅkhalapravṛttau kālidāsakavau asūyādoṣaḥ prakṛtakavinā..anusandheyam'. (p.4).

The commentaries on the Sanskrit dramas are therefore very important and the contribution that the commentators make to our knowledge and understanding of dramaturgy, poetics, history of Sanskrit classical and lexicographical literature and finally to textual criticism is really considerable. Many commentaries have not been as yet published and are available in manuscript form in the different libraries. These commentaries have to be published. These commentaries, whether published or unpublished deserve greater attention and a more sympathetic appreciation. One cannot help thinking that the present trend noticeable in many quarters of bringing out editions of dramas without the Prākrits and also without any commentary is indeed to be very much deplored. The view that the Sanskrit commentators only give word for word bare explanations is an utterly mistaken one and a critical study of many commentaries will reveal that even from the modern point of view, the modern canons of literary criticism, these commentators are really very good 'critics'. Rāghavabhaṭṭa, Pūrṇasarasvatī, Jagaddhara are some of the names of which we could be justly proud.

The commentaries selected for study here are the Rasamañjarī by Pūrṇasarasvatī on the Mālatimādhava, the Arthadyotanikā by Rāghavabhaṭṭa on the Abhijñānaśākuntala and the Abhijñānaśākuntalacarcā by an anonymous writer on the same play, the Saṁjīvana by Ghanaśyāma on the Uttararāmacarita, the Camatkārataraṅgiṇī by Sundarī and Kamalā on the Viddhaśālabhañjikā and the Diṅmātradarśinī on the Bhagavadajjukīya. This selection is made deliberately with a view to securing a sort of comprehensiveness and as much variety as possible in such a monograph. Here are represented ladies along with the men. The important forms from amongst the recognised ten forms, the Prakaraṇa, the Nāṭaka, the Nāṭikā, and the Prahasana find a place here. Two commentaries are on the same play, the Abhijñānaśākuntala, so that this should give an opportunity for a comparative study of the two expositions. Rāghavabhaṭṭa is a scholar while in Ghanaśyāma we have a minister at a court and in Pūrṇasarasvatī we have an ascetic and Sundarī and Kamalā are very learned co-wives. Lastly, Rāghavabhaṭṭa studied and wrote in that great centre of learning, Vārāṇasī in the North while Ghanśyāma wrote at Tanjore in the South. Kamalā and Sundarī are from Mahārāshtra while Pūrṇasarasvatī and the two anonymous authors hail from Kerala. These commentaries, one may feel, undoubtedly proclaim the individual and also reflect the atmosphere and traditions perhaps of the, land they hail from. The pleasing maturity and profundity of Rāghavabhaṭṭa, the haughty scholarship of Ghanaśyāma, the winsome modesty and confidence of Kamalā and Sundarī and the devotional mysticism of Pūrṇasarasvatī and his two comrades are qualities that these individuals seem to have inhaled and imbibed from the distinctive atmosphere and traditions in which they drew their breath.

II. THE RASAMAÑJARĪ

(Pūrṇasarasvatī on the Mālatīmādhava of Bhavabhūti)

The popular dictum that 'uttare rāmacarite bhavabhūtiḥ viśiṣyate' is certainly valid but the Mālatīmādhava too is no mean performance by Bhavabhūti. In several ways and in many respects it marks a remarkable improvement over the Mahāvīracarita, his first play and the Mālatīmādhava makes a critical student anticipate his Uttararāmacarita. Poetical thoughts are here splendidly expressed both in a polished prose and fine melodious verse, in a far better manner than has been done in the Mahāvīracarita and in many verses a listening ear can hear the echoes of the melody and the music of the Uttararāmacarita. In the Mahāvīracarita, Bhavabhūti thinks of a plot but cannot get over artificiality and he has not been able to make the plot move on account of the characters involved in it. This artistic welding of the characters and the plot, which makes things look inevitable, is much better done in the Mālatīmādhava and perfection in this respect is reached in the Uttararāmacarita. In the Mahāvīracarita and the Uttararāmacarita Bhavabhūti deals with the Rāma story but in the Mālatīmādhava he deals with a social theme, a story of love of two children of ministers at a royal court. He handles the spacious form of drama, the Prakaraṇa, which with its ten acts affords him ample scope for introducing a rich variety of incidents and characters and he has also tried to combine the contemporary with the imaginary in the making of his plot. The characters are drawn with commendable skill and it is no exaggeration to say that Bhavabhūti has given to Sanskrit literature unforgettable romantic lovers in his Mādhava and Mālatī and also in his Makaranda and Madayantikā. These characters are lively ones, remarkably poetic and immensly gain in effect on account of the contrast that they are made to offer each other. One would perhaps be justified in thinking that Makaranda and Madayantikā, the leading figures in the Patākā, the subplot, have a greater appeal for us on account of their boldness and vivacity and naturally interest us more than their counterparts in the Ādhikārika, the main story, Mādhava and Mālatī do, since these latter appear as suffering from a certain inactivity and shyness. In the young scholar with a poetic temperament, driven to desperateness as Mādhava, the hero, is presented to us, is perhaps to be seen the projection of the self and, therefore, the image of the poet himself. This is a hazardous guess but a tempting ene; the more one reads the play the more is one inclined to accept the possibility of the presence of autobiographical material in it.

In the very nature of things, one cannot be very dogmatic about this autobiographical element in the play, but one does get a very pleasant surprise when a Sanskrit commentator tries to understand the play as an allegory and makes a conscious effort to explain his idea in a very systematic manner. The Mālatīmādhava has been commented upon by three learned commentators, Tripurāri, Jagaddhara and Pūrṇasarasvatī. Tripurāri left his commentary incomplete and it was completed by his pupil Nānyadeva. All these commentaries are valuable for a proper appreciation of the play, its poetry and its suggestions. It is Pūrṇasarasvatī who is seen offering us a very ingenious suggestion regarding the allegory in this play. Towards the end of his commentary Pūrṇasarasvatī observes:

> 'atra mādhava iti sākṣāt lakṣmīpatiḥ nārāyaṇaḥ ucyate / śṛṅgāraḥ viṣṇudaivatyaḥ iti vacanāt śṛṅgāradevatā bhagavānevātra nāyakaḥ iti anusandhānārtham / mālatī tu saukumārya-saurabhyādiyogāt lakṣmīḥ / devaratā iti devaiḥ bhagavadavatāritārtham bhūmāvavatāritvāt kāśyapaḥ / bhūrivasu iti ananta-ratnākaratvāt kṣīrasāgaraḥ / makaranda iti 'rasaḥ vai saḥ' ityādi vacanāt paramānandarūpaḥ parameśvaraḥ / madayantikā iti mahāmāyātvena jaganmohanāt bhavānī / kāmandakī iti kāmitārtha-dānasāmarthyāt bhaktiḥ / buddharakṣitā iti buddhaiḥ vidvadbhiḥ paripālitatvāt sarasvatī / avalokitā iti prekṣāvadbhiḥ samyagālocitatvāt nītiḥ / lavaṅgikā iti parimalabahalatvatkīrtiḥ / kalahaṁsa iti madhurāvya

kta-uccāraḥ paramātmamantraḥ / aghoraghaṇṭa iti aśāstra-vihita-hiṁsāparatvāt adharmaḥ / kapālakuṇḍalā iti hiṁsā / saudāminī iti prakāśātmikā jhaṭiti sphuraṇena sakala-andhakārapaṭala-vighaṭana-paṭīyasī vidyā ityādi upāsanopāyuktā vāsanāpi mahākaveḥ daiṣṭikaiḥ anusandheyā iti sakalamatimaṅgalam' / (p. 621).

Thus would Pūrṇasarasvatī like to interpret the play : Devarāta and Bhūrivasu are Kaśyapa and the Kṣīrasāgara respectively and Mādhava, son to Kaśyapa is Viṣṇu while Mālatī, the daughter of Bhūrivasu is Lakṣmī. The 'rasa' in this play is Śṛṅgāra, which according to the works on dramaturgy has as its presiding deity Viṣṇu and therefore it would be in the fitness of things if the play has Viṣṇu as its hero, the 'nāyaka'. The name Mādhava is from this point of view very significant. Makaranda is Lord Śiva and Madayantikā is naturally Bhavānī. Buddharakṣitā is zealously guarded by the wise, hence Sarasvatī, Knowledge while Avalokitā as the name would suggest is Nīti, good ethical conduct. Kāmandakī is Bhakti with adequate power to grant wishes. Lavaṅgikā is the spreading fragrant fame while Kalahaṁsa is the sacred chant for the Lord. Saudāminī is the saving lore that with its flashes destroys the darkness of ignorance. In this manner Kāmandakī, Buddharakṣitā, Avalokitā and Saudāminī form the auspicious group of Sarasvatī, Bhakti, Nīti and Vidyā and together with Kalahaṁsa and Lavaṅgikā, the sacred chant and glorious fame, represent all that is religious, auspicious and sacred in life, Knowledge, Devotion, Good Conduct, sacred and sweet Spells that sing the glories of the Lord and it is these forces that ultimately win and witness the union of Viṣṇu and Lakṣmī and of Śiva and Bhavānī. The opposing forces, naturally are irreligious, being forces that often represent mistaken notions about religion and spiritual excellence, hence Aghoraghaṇṭa is Adharma incarnate while Kapālakuṇḍalā associated with him is abhorrent Hiṁsā. Saudāminī, the flashing Lightning that shows the way when darkness gathers is the Conscience which dispelling the darkness in the Soul, leads it onwards towards the realization of the Lord. In this manner, in one and the same play Bhavabhūti tried to depict the union of Hari with Lakṣmī and of Hara with Pārvatī. Bhakti and the other complimentary forces play the same important part and are sheer necessities in Vaiṣṇavism as well as in Śaivism.

Who would not say that the scheme of Pūrṇasarasvatī as explained here is not very clever and ingenious? The correspondence, as he points out, is complete in its own way. It is also that mythology describes both Lakṣmī and Bhavānī in much the same manner in which Bhavabhūti presents to us his Mālatī and Madayantikā. One is calm, serene and gentle while the other is vivacious, determined and all action. It is also interesting to see another commentator Jagaddhara remarking in the context of the hero Mādhava and his presentation to us by Bhavabhūti that:

> "Mādhava iti nāmnā śṛṅgāramayatā uktā / vasantasya ṣṛṅgāramayatvāt / śṛṅgāramayatvena viṣṇudaivatvam api kaṭākṣitam / yadāha bharataḥ :—'śṛṅgāraḥ viṣṇudaivataḥ' iti / ata eva śyāmatvam api vakṣyati' kuvalayadalaśyāmaḥ api aṅgam ityādinā / śyamo bhavet tu śṛṅgāraḥ ityapi bharataḥ /"

From these remarks it would appear that the commentators appear to think that Bhavabhūti had possibly some such idea in his mind when he thought of his hero, his name and his complexion. It could be easily conceded that Bhavabhūti appears to have had some definite plan and idea when he thought of the names of his characters in this play, since the names of some of his characters like Kāmandakī, Buddharakṣitā, Avalokitā, Saudāminī are indeed transparent and offer us some clue to the leading concept behind the character. Jagaddhara tries to explain these names and while attempting to do so he has to observe :

> "Kāmandakī nītigranthabhedaḥ tam vetti iti kāmandakī / 'tadāhite' ityāṅ, ṅīp ca / anayā nāmavyutpattyā nītiveditabodhanena prakṛta-siddhi-hetutā uktā / tadantevāsini avalokitadṛṣṭiḥ iti kāryasiddhi-dṛṣṭer api kāryasiddhihetutā uktā taduttejanikā iti / ..aghoraghaṇṭa kāpālikā-

stu ghaṇṭāntanāmānaḥ samudāḥrtāḥ iti bharataḥ / aghoraḥ avimṛśyakārīti nāmavyutpattiḥ / ..makarandaḥ puṣparasaḥ kalahaṁsaḥ rājahaṁsaḥ /"

In his commentary Jagaddhara reveals that he too is inclined to read in the Mālatīmādhava an allegory. His observations at several places in which he tries to make his ideas clear could be brought together and it would seem that he is trying to read in the play an idea somewhat systematically developed. His remarks relevant in this context are :

"..ata eva jaladakālam anubhāvyaivaitatprakaraṇavṛttānta iti dhvanitam / ...nanu mālatīvallabhatvam mādhavasya na yogyam vasantena samaṁ varṣākālīnayā mālatyā jāteḥ sambandhābhāvāt / apūrvam eva hi padārthasārtham yoginīprabhāvāt sampannam āsādya sahṛdayahṛdayacamatkārakāriṇīm vaidagdhīm eva kavir ayam utprekṣitavān iti adoṣaḥ / mādhava iti śṛngāramayatā uktā / vasantasya śṛngāramayatvāt / śṛṅgāramayatvena viṣṇudaivatvam api kaṭākṣitam / yad āha bharataḥ-śṛṅgāraḥ viṣṇudaivataḥ iti / ata eva śyāmatvam api vakṣyati 'kuvalayadalaśyāmo' pyaṅgam' ityādinā / śyāmo bhavettu śṛṅgāraḥ ityapi bharataḥ / ...kalahaṁsaḥ rājahaṁsaḥ sa ca śaradi vīragamano'pi yoginīprabhāvāt vasante militaḥ itināmābhiprāyaḥ / ..mādhavasya vasantasya makarandaḥ puṣparasaḥ sahacaraḥ yujyate eva/atra makarandena puṣparasena sahacaraḥ mādhavaḥ vasantaḥ bālabakulam alaṅkaroti iti dhvanir api unmiṣati /"

From these remarks of Jagaddhara one is able to gather that according to him, Bhavabhūti had in his mind some theme from Nature when he thought of the plot of this play as well as the names and the peculiar dispositions of his characters. The unusual and therefore miraculous blooming of the Mālatī creeper in the Vasanta season, though as a matter of fact the Mālatī blooms only in the rainy season appears, to have been the leading idea in Bhavabhūti's mind. Mādhava, Makaranda and Kalahaṁsa represent the Vasanta season and its associates, the forces that strengthen it and make the atmosphere intoxicating, while Mālatī and Lavaṅgikā represent the delicate creepers of the rainy season, creepers that fill in the atmosphere by their sweet aroma in a pleasant manner without having anything dazzling about them. Saudāminī would obviously suggest the atmosphere of the rainy season while Kāmandakī along with Buddharakṣitā and Avalokitā would represent that carefully, zealously guarded benevolent magic which brings about this miracle of the union of Mādhava and Mālatī, the Vasanta and the Jāti. The two other characters of Makaranda and Madayantikā, honey and the intoxicating atmosphere only serve to heighten the effect of the beauty of Vasanta. Jagaddhara reads the suggestion of the 'jaladakāla' in the Nāndī verse itself in the words 'murajarava'. The play, in some such manner is a wonderful story, 'ramaṇīya, vicitra, ujjvala prakaraṇa' in which the pure sweet Jāti, natural to the rainy season, gets attached to the intoxicating Vasanta with the attending maddening atmosphere of sweet cooings, honey and the like. The allegory that Jagaddhara finds in the play can be described as 'Natural' to distinguish it from the 'Philosophical' one that has been suggested by Pūrṇasarasvatī.

It will be possible for us to understand in the light of this discussion of the commentators, the reasons why Bhavabhūti has not been quite successful in the construction as well as in the conduct of his plot in this play. It appears that on account of the presence of some such diverse ideas present in his mind when he constructed his social play with its romance developed along the lines of the Kāmasūtra, not only his canvass became crowded but his concepts also became somewhat clouded and in some measure confused too, being subjected to the varying influences of a diverse nature, namely those of Polity, Religion, Nature and finally the Kāmasūtra. All these different strains and pulls on Bhavabhūti's mind when he wrote this play are clearly visible in the play as it stands and this is the chief reason why the welding of the plot is not what it ought to have been and as a consequence of which the play suffers from a certain lack of unity. The ideas are really clever and one can understand the feelings of satisfaction which

Bhavabhūti expresses in his remarks towards the close of his play

"Asti vā kutaścid evambhūtam mahādbhutaṁ vicitra-ramaṇīyojjvalaṁ prakaraṇam" /

Pūrṇasarasvatī who has been very much impressed by the performance of Bhavabhūti in this play significantly comments in the following manner:

"Anayā ca uktibhaṅgyā
yasya deve parā bhaktiḥ yathā deve tathā gurau /
tasyaite kathitāhy arthāḥ prakāśante mahātmanaḥ //
iti śrutivacananityā devaguruprasādaparimṛditakaṣāyatayā prādurbhūta-śabdabrahmaṣāmrājyam svahṛdayānurūpam parisamāpitaprāyaḥ prārabdhaprakaraṇaḥ paṇḍitavidagdhamaṇḍalamuṇḍamaṇḍanamahāmaṇiḥ mahākaviḥ ātmanaḥ prakaraṇākhyarūpakaviśeṣasaṁvidhānacāturīṁ sahṛdayān prati prakāśayati / evambhutam mālatīmadhavākhyaprakaraṇaprakārayuktam evambhūtam punarevaṃ kṛtamityuktyā prakaraṇanirmāṇāya svasmin saṁrambhiṇī gurudevatāprasādapauruṣasyeva tasya yatnataḥ prādurbhūtatvam ātmanaḥ tatra ahamabhimānarāhityāt avikatthanatām ca vyañjayati" / (p. 612-613).

Inspiration for an allegory as well as an understanding of the same- both are to some extent rewards of scholarship and piety as the commentator Pūrṇasarasvatī would like to suggest here. It could be very easily conceded that these are very happy moments both for the artist and the critic. There is a certain spontaneous element in both these processes, the one in the artist, and the other in the critic. But it also must be borne in mind while attempting to bring out the 'dhvani' or the ultimate meaning sought to be conveyed, one has to be very cautious in not overdoing the thing and Tripurāri has some very significant observations to make in this context:

"iti kecid vyācakṣate / tad etacchabdaśaktyā pratīyate arthaśaktyā vā iti te eva jānanti / na tu ete śabdāḥ prakṛtārthaniyantritā api śaktyantarabalāt anvitamarthāntaram pratyāyayanti iti kasyacit vyutpannasya pratītiḥ / artho'pi prakṛto naitādṛśasya arthāntarasya pratītau samarthaḥ anubhūyate sahṛdayaiḥ / kathāṁśānām eva nirvahaṇe nirūpyamāṇānām mukhasandhau sūcanānirbandhaḥ / na tu tatra vakṣyamāṇasya sarvartuvanavarṇanādeḥm api / tataḥ naiṣo' rthaḥ kaveḥ vivakṣāgocaro' pi/ tasmān na ayam dhvanimārgavidām panthāḥ /" (p.3)

Tripurāri is here criticising Jagaddhara for his interpretation of the verse 'sānandaṁ nandihasta' etc. MM. I. 2. where he reads the various details of the rainy season suggested, for Jagaddhara after having explained the verse in his own manner observes 'ata eva jaladakālamanubhāvyaitatprakāraṇavṛttānta iti dhvanitam'. Even though one is in favour of accepting Jagaddhara's interpretation, one has to concede that the remarks of Tripurāri are extremely valuable for all criticism that seeks to interpret great works of literary art. A critic too, has, like the poet, his own personality and this personality is bound to influence his approach to the work of art he studies. Tripurāri, as well as Jagaddhara and Pūrṇasarasvatī are all good scholars, for Tripurāri describes himself as 'sāhitya-adhva-parikṣuṇṇadhiyām asmādṛśām' while Jagaddhara describes himself as one who had mastery over Nyāya of Gotama, Grammar of Pāṇini, Koṣas and Kāvyas, Chandas and Alaṅkāra, and finally Bharata and the Śrutis. Jagaddhara speaks thus :

> "Yenāpāṭhi kaṭhoragautamamunerṁ vaiśeṣikaṁ khaṇḍanam, yenāśrāvi sakoṣakāvyanivahaṁ tatpāṇinīyam matam / chando'laṅkaraṇaṁ ca bhavyabharataṁ yenādhyagāmi śrutistasyāmuṣya jagaddharasya kavituṣṭikeyam ujjṛmbhatām // (p. 124)

Pūrṇasarasvatī too was a scholar like Tripurāri and Jagaddhara, no doubt, but he was of a philosophic bent of mind and this fact to my mind does explain his attempt to read a 'philosophical allegory' in the play. He tells us about himself in his introduction to the play 'Kamalinīrājahaṁsa' nāṭaka thus:

> "tad idānīṁ viṣadaviśrutavinayamādhuryadhuryeṇa parameśvarabhaktisārasīvihārakāsāreṇa padavākyapramāṇanetratrayanirīkṣaṇaparaparameśvarapūrṇajyotirmunīvaranihita nissṛtakaruṇāmṛtapūrṇacandreṇa pūrṇasarasvatīnāmadheyena kavinā nibaddham.."

Whether one is convinced or not with what Pūrṇasarasvatī has to say of this play, the Mālatīmādhava, yet one would be justified in saying that in him both the play and Bhavabhūti have found a clever interpreter.

The commentary of Pūrṇasarasvatī has very happily been named as 'Rasamañjarī', for it not only enables us to appreciate the play it seeks to elucidate but in itself also is a remarkable piece of literary art and composition. Like Vīrarāghava and Rāghavabhaṭṭa he has remarkable poetic qualities in him and this is amply reflected in his commentary. His very wide reading in literature is to be seen as reflected in the wide range of the quotations with which he regals us. He has a very high regard for Bhavabhūti and he loses no opportunity of paying him compliments in choice phrases, To him. Bhavabhūti is a 'lord of the poets' 'Kavīśvara' (89, 103, 108, 174, 594); a poet with great skill and one very adept in the delineation of sentiments, 'rasasudhāsamvidhānasāvadhānaḥ (108)'. The other epithets are 'sahṛdayacamatkārakārikaviparameśvara(122), kavikulacakravarti (205), kavikulamukunda(383), rasasaṁvidhānaratnanidhānabhūta mahākavi (611), and 'paṇḍitavidagdhamaṇḍalamuṇḍamaṇḍanamahāmaṇi mahākavi (613)! Though he thus appears to be an ardent admirer of Bhavabhūti, yet he has judiciously read and mastered the works of Kālidāsa, Māgha and others, the two Epics, Prākrit poems like the Setubandha and he also reveals his close study of works on dramaturgy, rhetorics and the Kāmasūtra. As a consequence, his commentary reveals his critical insight and literary abilities.

As a commentator out to point out the excellences of the work he so much likes, he takes care to point out the 'dhvani' at several places and he quotes also from the Dhvanikāra. (11). He notices that the verse I. 10 cd—'prāṇais tapobhirathavābhimatairmadīyaiḥ kṛtyam ghaṭeta suhṛdaḥ yadi tatkṛtam syāt'—has in it the 'vyatireka—alaṅkāradhvani' (39). He has to observe that 'sarvam hi saudāminyāḥ sambhāvyate' has in it the word 'saudāminī' significantly used, has in that word the 'arthāntarasaṅkramita vācya dhvani' and suggests her being one possessed of all the good and miraculous powers, 'sarvaguṇasampatpātratva' (50). While commenting on the celebrated passage "tasyām abhinavo vicitraḥ kusumeṣu-vyāpāraḥ tadbhavatu kṛtārthatā vaidagdhasya, phalatu nirmāṇam ramaṇīyatāyāḥ vidhātuḥ samāsādayatu sarasa eva bhartṛdārikāyāḥ kaṇṭhāvalambanamahārghatām iti" he points out that here we have the 'śabdaśaktimūla vastudhvani'. This is not a case of 'śleṣa alaṅkāra'. He observes "śabdaśaktimūlo vastudhvanirayam na punaḥ śleṣālaṅkāraḥ / ubhayorapyartha yoḥ tatra vācyatvāt / atra tu ekasyaiva vācyatvāt parasya vyaṅgyatvāt ca" // (84). In this manner he assists us in understanding the text as well as the 'dhvani' intended by the poet. Often times Pūrṇasarasvatī uses the forms 'iti dhvaniḥ, iti dhvanitam, dhvanyate, dyotyate, sūcayati' etc.

This same care that is seen in this study of the 'dhvani' is also seen in his 'rasa' analysis of the play. Bhavabhūti himself tells us that his play is a remarkable composition, for he has very skilfully used the 'rasa' in a diverse manner, 'bhūmnā rasānām gahanāḥ prayogāḥ' I. 6. and therefore perhaps we find Pūrṇasarasvatī pointing out the 'rasa' and its various 'bhāvas' almost everywhere and at all the very significant places, without fail. He points out the 'śṛṅgāra, vīra, karuṇa, adbhuta, bhayānaka, raudra' at their proper places indicating also the attending paraphernalia of other contributory emotions as used by the poet. He has been careful in noticing the use of the different Vṛttis like the Ārabhaṭī (198) and the Kaiśikī (78) in the context of the Rasas the 'raudra, bībhatsa and śṛṅgāra' respectively. For his analysis of the delineation of an emotion and its expression, one may refer to his comments on I. 30. Bhavabhūti's verse is

> "stimitavikasitānām ullasadbhrūlatānām masṛṇamukulitānām prāntavistārabhājām /

pratinayananipāte kiñcidākuñcitānām vividham aham
abhūvam pātram ālokitānām //

Pūrṇasarasvatī observing that the poet here uses the glances as advised by Bharata for developing the 'śṛṅgāra-bharatoktānām navarasopayoginīnām dṛṣṭīnām madhye' catuṣṣaṣṭidṛṣṭayaḥ śṛṅgāropayoginyaḥ tāsu kāścit prakāśyante' explains the 'dṛṣṭis' in the light of the discussion in the Bhāvaprakāśa. It is significant to note that he connects the 'dṛṣṭis' with the 'anubhāvas' thus : stimita with vismaya, vikasita with harṣa, ullasad-bhrū with adbhuta or prāpticintā, masṛṇa with anurāga, mukulita with sukha and moha as well, ākuñcita with lajjā and so on. He has referred to Māgha and Kālidāsa in his discussion of the 'ardhamukulita dṛṣṭi' and the' pratinayananipāta kiñcidākuñcita' showing the parallels from their works. He notices the 'svabhāvokti alaṅkāra' and draws our attention pointedly towards the 'rasa' delineation by reminding us that 'atra ca bhūmna rasānām gahanāḥ prayogāḥ' iti pratijñātasya yojanam anusandheyam'. (pp. 73-75). Pūrṇasarasvatī is quick to point out that the apparent repetition in v. 30,

"asāraṁ saṁsāram parimuṣitaratnaṁ tribhuvanaṁ
nirālokaṁ lokaṁ maraṇaśaranaṁ bāndhavajanam /
adarpaṁ kandarpam jananayananirmāṇamaphalaṁ
jagajjīrṇāraṇyam katham asi vidhātuṁ vyavasitaḥ //"
MM. v. 30

is no fault and indeed is to be regarded as an excellence since it only contributes to the development of the Karuṇa rasa that is suggested. He properly studies the emotions behind this expression and points out that the speaker here has two emotions in him, one, the love for his beloved and the other, anger for his enemy and with his mind full of these two strong emotions he has thus expressed himself. He observes :

"saṁsārādīnām uddeśyānām asāratvādīnām vidheyānām paryāyatve'pi punaḥ yaduktiḥ priyānurāgaripuroṣavivaśacetaso vakturna kevalaṁ na doṣaḥ api tu guṇa eva iti mantavyam / 'doṣo' pi guṇaḥ kvacit kvacinnobhāv-iti kāvyaprakāśokteḥ / 'aviśeṣeṇa pūrvoktaṁ yadi bhūyo' pi kīrtyate / tad ekārthaṁ rasākṣiptacetasām tanna duṣyati / iti bhojavacanācca / ...atra karuṇaraso dhvanyate / (p. 312)"

He has drawn support for his contention from Mammaṭa and Bhoja and it is to be further seen that he has entered into a discussion regarding the 'alaṅkāra', here, 'mālānidarśanā' and 'atiśayokti' giving his reasons. Pūrṇasaravatī has been throughout careful in pointing out the rise and development of emotions in not only the principal characters like Mālatī, Mādhava, Makaranda and Madayantikā but also in animals and the like and one may refer in this context to ix. 32. which describes the love-making of an elephant :

"Kaṇḍūkuḍmaliteksaṇāṁ sahacarīṁ dantasya koṭyā likhan / paryāyavyatikīrṇakarṇapavanairāhlādibhirvījayan / jagdhārdhairnavasallakīkisalayairasyāḥ sthitiṁ kalpayan dhanyo vanyamataṅgajaḥ paricayaprārambham abhyasyati //
ix. 32.

Pūrṇasarasvatī in his comments here is very clever no doubt, as he has brought out all the suggestions intended by Bhavabhūti. Thus the singular 'dantasya' suggests the close standing of the two, the elephant and his mate with mouth pretty close (dantasya na punaḥ dantayoḥ ityanena parasparasaṁśliṣtapārśvayoḥ dvayoḥ ghaṭitamukhatvena sthitiḥ sūcyate) and 'kuḍmaliteksaṇā' suggests the 'happiness' experienced by the mate (dantakoṭilekhanasukhānubhūti). The word 'sahacarī' indicates the beloved who does not bear any separation even for a moment (sahacarīṁ kṣaṇamapi virahāsahāṁ priyām iti viśeṣaṇaiva viśeṣyaṁ siddhyati) and 'likhan' suggests a fond and loving 'scratching (yathāsukhaṁ kaṇḍūyanaṁ vyajyate). Again the word 'jagdhārdhaiḥ' suggests that the male is offering only the 'sweetest bits' to his beloved after personally examining them (jagdhārdhaiḥ svayaṁ carvitaikadeśairiti svādiṣṭhaṁ svādiṣṭhaṁ nirūpya iti dyotyate). The fact that the elephant is 'vanya' indicates his freedom without any restraints (vanyaḥ vane bhavaḥ iti niryantraṇavilasitatvam khyāpyate). The verb 'abhyasyati' i.e. practices suggests that the elephant is a young one and is indulging in love only newly. (abhyasatītyanena kalabhatvāt navapravṛtta sambhogatvamāha). Finally Pūrṇasarasvatī concludes his comments by pointing out that here we have the 'bhāva' delight, 'harṣa' and also 'sambhogaśṛṅgāra'. He also observes that the 'alaṅkāra' is 'svabhāvokti'. One could be really grateful to the commentator for all this help for properly understanding a verse where, after all, the simplicity is so deceptive. He has taken care to point out the 'bhavasandhis' also and has indulged into discussions about the Alaṅkāra almost everywhere often quoting authorities in support. It would be no exaggeration to say that the Mālatīmādhava is a study in Rasa and Alaṅkāra by Bhavabhūti and Pūrṇasarasvatī offers us all possible assistance in understanding Bhavabhūti in this respect.

His dramaturgic discussions are equally illuminating and he has in his commentary pointed out the different Sandhis with their Sandhyaṅgas. The reader, however, is to be careful in following and understanding this analysis, for, Pūrṇasarasvatī does not introduce his discussion by the formula used by Rāghavabhaṭṭa and others-'anena..aṅgam uktam' etc. One may in this context refer to his discussions on the Sandhis and the five Avasthās, the sixty-four Sandhyaṅgas and their purpose in a drama as well as the locating of the Upakṣepa and the Parinyāsa, the two opening aṅgas of the Mukhasandhi. He observes that he would be pointing out the various Sandhyaṅgas at their proper places-'sandhyaṅgāni ca tatra tatra yojayiṣyāmaḥ'. (p. 36). He shows acquaintance with the different forms of the Sanskrit drama (p. 613) and also for us summarises the suggestions of a Viṣkambhaka (p, 323) and also discusses the Nāndī at length. (4-6). He carries on his discussions with quotations from Bharata, Dhanañjaya, Dhanika, Śāradātanaya and suggests that Bādarāyaṇa was a writer on dramaturgy, since he quotes his views on the Nāndī. (p.5). A curious authority he quotes from is Bhaṭṭaghasyu while explaining the word Nāndī. It could, therefore, be said that Pūrṇasarasvatī examines the play according to the canons of dramaturgy as he tries to understand its poetry after the rhetoricians like Vāmana, Daṇḍin, Ānandavardhana and Bhoja.

What strikes a critical reader of Pūrṇasarasvatī is the very large number of the religious and philosophical texts from which he quotes. The Āgama, the Upaniṣads like the Taittirīya, the Chāndoyga, the Kena, and the Bṛhadāraṇyaka, the Gītā, the Brahmasūtras, the Śvetāśvatara Upaniṣad, the Yogasūtras, the Nyāyadīpāvalī, Manusmṛti and finally the Mahābhārata are often referred to. A commentary on a love play replete with such references clearly reveals the philosophical temperament of the author and one can hence understand the allegorical explanation of the play that he has offered as perfectly natural so far as he is concerned.

But what is of greater importance is the fact that his philosophy and devotion did not make him blind or insensitive to the poetic beauties and clever suggestions in the play. Everywhere one finds Pūrṇasarasvatī bringing out the suggestions, implications and the appropriateness of the elegant and subtle expressions of Bhavabhūti. One is tempted to refer to his comments on IX. 27 in this context. Bhavabhūti's verse is :

> "naveṣu lodhraprasaveṣu kāntiḥ dṛśaḥ kuraṅgeṣu gataṁ gajeṣu /
> latāsu namratvam iti pramathya vyaktaṁ vibhaktā vipine priyā me //

A Sanskrit reader would not here expect to be much assisted by any commentator in the appreciation of this simple yet elegant composition, as he would need no explanation and yet we find the poet in Pūrṇasarasvatī making significant comments on almost every phrase. Drawing on parallels to establish the connection between the Lodhra and the whiteness, he adds that Mālatī is also 'pale and white', lovelorn as she is (tasyāḥ smarapāṇḍutvāt). 'gataṁ gajeṣu' is explained by him as suggesting so many graces of Mālatī, her beautiful form, her consciousness of her youth and her emotion of love and the graceful langour about her, (gatam gamanam gajeṣu nitambādigauravāt, yauvanamadanagarvāt ca, līlā-alasatvāt ca) and he does succeed in creating before us a very happy picture of the lady. And in a Kālidasian manner he explains 'latāsu namratvam' as 'aśokalatikādiṣu namratvam namanaśīlatvam, stanastabakāvarjitatvāt, 'āvarjitā kiñcidiva stanābhyām' iti, stanābhirāmastabakāvanamrām' ityādiprayogāt). One may refer to yet another place. In Act vi. Mālatī embraces Mādhava thinking him to be Lavaṅgikā and observes : 'iyam āliṅgāmi / darśanam punaḥ bāṣpotpīḍena priyasakhyā apaścimam na labhyate / (āliṅgya sānandam)'. Her sight is rendered ineffective by the swelling tears and yet she feels joy at the touch and hence this expression of joy. Pūrṇasarasvatī adds here that the touch of the dearest is always, even if the person is not seen, the cause of great happiness and in support refers to the Uttararāmacarita and the Raghuvaṁśa. He observes ; 'adarśane'pi sparśāntarāt priyatamasparśanasya saviśeṣasukhapradatvam svabhāvataḥ anusandhāya āha-yathā uttararāmacarite bhāgīrathīvarāntarhitāyāḥ sītādevyāḥ sparśe rāmaḥ 'iyam gṛhyase' iti, raghuvaṁśe ca, 'vispaṣṭamasrāndhatayā na dṛṣṭau jñātau sutasparśasukhopalambhāt iti'. Pūrṇasarasvatī is always drawing on parallels from other poets and in the process reveals his own fine poetical sensitivities, sahṛdayatva and rasikatva. His comments on V. 8. :

> "avimuktamadgrathitakesarāvalīsatatadhīvaśasubhagārpitastanaḥ /
> api karṇajahāviniveśitānanāḥ priyayā tadaṅgaparivṛttim āpnuyām" //

evoke our admiration, since they come from an ascetic, as the word 'sarasvatī' in his name would indicate. In this verse Mādhava is expressing his keen longing for an embrace, 'aṅga-parivṛtti' with Mālati and Pūrṇasarasvatī fully explains the idea involved and observes that this is the embrace, the Upagūhana called Tilataṇḍula by Vātsyāyana and quotes from him. What a different spirit altogether did this ascetic possess from that of the scholar Ghanaśyāma!

It is no wonder if this fine ascetic possessed a charming style. One is pleasantly struck by his poetry and his soft alliterative phrases. He renders Bhavabhūti's 'dāritarasātalaḥ prapātaḥ' as 'līlāpāṭavidalitadharaṇitalaḥ (p. 495); Bhavabhūti's 'katham avalokayeyam' IX. 1 18 (p. 515) as 'sarvendriyaduḥkhadāyinīnāmāsāmāvalokanameva rauravapatanabhairavam kim punaranubhavanam' happily bringing out the intense sorrow and the pangs of Mādhava. In a similar manner we see Bhavabhūti's 'pramohamṛgatṛṣṇikā' in IX. 35 explained as 'ayam me suhṛd iyam me priyā ityanyathājñānarūpam marīcikam, marīcikatvāropaṇam jalabuddhyā vilobhitasya tṛṣitasya marudhārānipatitāsu madhyāhnamihiramarīcikāvīcikāsu mūḍhāpravṛttiriva mamāpi vanacareṣu gandhasindhurādiṣu bandhubuddhibandhanam iti dyotayati'. The familiar concept of the mirage is explained here, but the poetic diction deserves our notice. Pūrṇasarasvatī often makes his explanation lucid and interesting by adding a few illustrations of his own: thus while explaining Bhavabhūti's IX. 36 'tvayyāpado gaṇayatā svayamanvabhāvi', a case of fears coming true, Pūrṇasarasvatī observes in his own style 'yathā jhaṭiti paṭu raṭati jaladharapaṭale sphuṭamaśaniḥ śanairmama śirasi patiṣyati iti śaṅkamānasya patite tasmin tadduḥkhānubhūtireveti bhāvaḥ/'bahuduḥkho nirduḥkhaḥ' iti lokavādam cānusandhatte '(p. 542). The 'pada-lālitya' here needs no comments. Again, while explaining Bhavabhūti's 'taṭasthaḥ svānarthān ghaṭayati ca maunaṁ ca bhajate' I. 17. (p. 44) Pūrṇasarasvatī points out that we do not have any 'lakṣaṇā' indication in 'taṭasthaḥ' and then adds 'yathā tīragataḥ eva bako matsyamanveti tameva kavalīkṛtya tūṣṇīmāste, tathā svayam dūrasthito' nanupraviṣṭa evetyarthaḥ'. He reveals his sense of humour in his explanation of 'makarandena niṣṭhuram abhihato jāmātā in Act. vii. (p. 386) when he observes 'nirdayam abhihataḥ gardabhena iva kṛtavyāyāmakaṭhinābhyām caraṇābhyām tāḍitaḥ'. Another interesting place is where he comments on Kāmandakī's expression of her desires and disappointments in X. 6. 'mayā na dṛṣṭastanayaḥ stanandhayaḥ' (p. 579). Pūrṇasarasvatī referring to her manifold desires, 'manorathānām bāhuvidhyam' refers to the 'old maiden's prayer for a groom' in 'let my sons eat and drink in plenty ghee and milk'—'putrā me saghṛtakṣiram bhuñjīran iti vṛddhakumarīvaraprārthanāvat.' In this respect Pūrṇasarasvatī resembles Rāghavabhaṭṭa who also often tries to make his point clear by new and happy analogies and illustrations of his own. In one respect, however, Pūrṇasarasvatī improves over Rāghavabhaṭṭa in that he often draws very apt parallels from the Epics and other poets.

One is tempted to feel it as natural that Pūrṇasarasvatī with his religious and philosophic bent of mind should regard' the marriage of Mādhava and Mālatī as of the 'Prājāpatya type and not of the 'Gāndharva' one as Jagaddhara holds. After discussing the meaning of vi. 18 Kāmandakī's advice to the young wedded ones, in 'śreyo mitram bandhutā vā samagrā' Pūrṇasarasvatī enters into a full discussion of this problem, quotes from the Smṛtis and then offers his conclusion that 'prājāpatyo'yam vivāho na tu gāndharva iti sūcitam' mainly relying on Manu, a conclusion which he has already given when he discusses this very matter in the context of Lavaṅgikā's advice to Mālatī to proceed boldly to secure her lover. (p. 118) in his emphatic 'nātra gāndharvo vivāho vidhīyate'. Pūrṇasarasvatī thinks that the Gāndharva form is meant only for the Kṣatriyas and not for the Brāhmins. Further, this marriage is, in fact, in accordance with the intentions of the parents. It is also blessed and brought about by their preceptor Kāmandakī. That the hero and the heroine have fallen in love with each other, parasparānukūla, is a laudable and pleasant circumstance no doubt, but that cannot make the form 'Gāndharva' as contemplated by the Smṛtis. This difference of views between Pūrṇasarasvatī and Jagaddhara not only indicates their independent thinking but also shows that these commentators did pay their attention to the social problems involved in works of art while discussing problems aesthetic, dramaturgical and rhetorical.

These commentators have also discussed the different readings and shown their preferences for particular readings with their reasons. One may in this context of 'textual criticism' refer by way of an illustration to VIII. 1. which runs:'..viyati pavanavegāt unmukhaḥ ketakīnām / abhinava iva sāndro mākarandaḥ..//'. Now, the Ketakī-kusuma has no 'madhu' honey in it as is clear from the verse,

"apasara madhukara dūram parimalabahule' pi ketakī-
kusume /
iha nahi madhukaṇalābho bhavati paraṁ dhūlidhūsa-
ram vadanam //"

and if this be correct then Bhavabhūti is obviously wrong in referring to 'ketakīnām sāndro mākarandaḥ parāgaḥ' here. Jagaddhara reads here 'mandamandam parāgaḥ' and so there is no difficulty for him. Nānyadeva reads the last line as 'pracalita iva sāndraḥ sphārasphāram parāgaḥ' and so for him also there is no difficulty. Pūrṇasarasvatī, however, has 'mākarandaḥ parāgaḥ' and therefore he indulges into a discussion to show that there is no contradiction, Virodha, involved here, since in the Ketakīkusuma too there is 'madhu', after all, it being a flower. (kusumatvaviśeṣādasyāpi madhusadbhāvo'styeva.). In the verse 'apasara madhukara' what is intended to convey is that his mouth would be soiled by the dust of pollen and so there would not be any acquisition of 'madhu'. There is no intention to convey the total absence of 'madhu' in the flower. 'apasara madhukara ityatrā' pi na madhvābhāvaḥ pratipādyate, tallābhasyaiva niṣidhyamānatvāt / tatra hetuḥ dhūlipālidhūsaritavadanatvam /'. One may or may not accept this defence of Bhavabhūti by Pūrṇasarasvatī, but one is pleased to find that the commentators did pay their attention to these problems. One may also refer to another case in this very context. We have the celebrated III. 16 which runs as

"kavalita iva kṛtsnaś cakṣuṣā sphāritena prasabham amṛtamegheneva sāndreṇa siktaḥ /
aviralamiva dāmnā pauṇḍarīkena naddhaḥ snapita iva ca dugdhasrotasā nirbhareṇa //"

Here both Tripurāri and Jagaddhara have the cd as ab and ab as cd. But Pūrṇasarasvatī remarks that his reading is correct since it accords well with both the immediate context and with the intentions of the poet. He observes: "asya ślokasya pūrvottarārdhayoḥ pāṭhavyatyāsaḥ prāmādikaḥ / yadahamatarkita ityādi vākyaśeṣasyāsambandhāt utprekṣānimittakathanapuraḥsaramevotprekṣaṇasya aucityāt / anyathā tasya ākasmikatvaprasaṅgāt madhyavartino hetoḥ purato 'nukarṣaṇasya asāmañjasyāt / snapita iva ca iti cakārasya sarvavākyārthasamuccāyinaścaramavākya eva kavinā tathā pāthacihnatvena prayuktatvāt vākyāntare tvaprayogāt ca /" It should be clear from this discussion that the Sanskrit commentators did not simply blindly comment on the text before them and went on simply giving other words for the original ones.

The authorities whom Pūrṇasarasvatī refers to are many and the number of quotations that he gives is really formidable. Even a casual glance at his commentary is sufficient to convince one of his scholarship and wide reading.

Appropriately enough, has Pūrṇasarasvatī named his commentary as 'Rasamañjarī' and none would deny him the compliment of having enabled a reader of the Mālatīmādhava to appreciate and understand Bhavabhūti in a better manner. A 'sahṛdaya' is likely to nod in assent to his very humble request in

> "mālatīmādhavasyoccaiḥ āmodam svam vivṛṇvatī /
> dhāryā sahṛdayaiḥ prītyā vyākhyeyam rasamañjarī //" (9.p.2)

for, here there is very little that could be regarded as a 'flaw in either diction or exposition, 'skhalitamiha yadi syāt arthataḥ śabdataḥ vā,' (7.p.2), nor is there any unnecessary 'expansion', 'prathanadoṣa'. It could safely be asserted that amongst the noted commentators of the Sanskrit dramas, Pūrṇasarasvatī, the 'sahṛdaya sannyāsin' has an assured place, combining in himself, as he does, very fine qualities rarely found together.

III. THE ARTHADYOTANIKĀ

(Rāghavabhaṭṭa on the Abhijñānaśākuntala of Kālidāsa)

In respects more than one does Rāghavabhaṭṭa reveal that his is a spirit akin to that of Pūrṇasarasvatī where we find a very happy blend of poetic sensitivity and scholarship. Rāghavabhaṭṭa chose to comment on what is universally regarded as the greatest of Sanskrit plays, the Abhijñānaśākuntala of the 'kavikulaguru' Kālidāsa and it could be said that he has given us a really commendable performance. Rāghavabhaṭṭa on the score of this performance could be described as a poet-commentator. Even the commentator Ghanaśyāma who boasts of being a 'poet of poets', 'kavīnāṁ kaviḥ', does not anywhere approach this fine performance of Rāghavabhaṭṭa, for Ghanaśyāma too had a similar opportunity when he chose to comment on the Uttararāmacarita of Bhavabhūti. Haughty Ghanaśyāma could not at all control the scholar in him, hence he simply could not enter into the spirit of the great play he had before him, a feat which the poet Rāghavabhaṭṭa could accomplish here. As a consequence, it has been possible for Rāghavabhaṭṭa to bring out everywhere whatever Kālidāsa wanted to convey both by expression and suggestion. He very rarely misses anything that is significant and at times one is tempted to give him due credit for having 'successfully painted the lily' a compliment which would be withheld in other cases.

Like his comrades in the field, Rāghavabhaṭṭa too was properly equipped for the task of explaining the Abhijñānaśākuntala. He tells us that he was a 'pada-vākya-pramāṇa-pārāvārīṇa', a 'sāhitya-ratnākara-sakala-kalā-śāstra-pravīṇa' and a 'nāṭya-alaṅkṛti-śāstra-tattvavit' and by any standards this is quite an impressive list of intellectual attainments. This is indeed amply corroborated by the internal evidence from the commentary itself but what strikes a reader of this commentary is the fact that this scholar was a 'rasika' and a 'sahṛdaya' who possessed in a rich measure the happy quality of 'tanmayībhavanayogyatā', a quality so necessary for a critic. His style, simple and facile, has a certain poetic glow and an easy eloquence, qualities on account of which he offers a sharp contrast to the other commentators who often seem to prefer the laconic style while commenting. Tripurāri tells us that his Bhāvapradīpikā has been deliberately composed in a laconic style. He observes:

"ato mitena vacasā laghvī bhāvapradīpikā /
mālatīmādhavasyeyam racyate rasikapriyā' //"
(p.1 BP on MM)

Ghanaśyāma tells us that he could spare and, therefore, pay little time to the composition of his commentary on the Uttararāmacarita. He is seen to observe :

"śrīrāmanavamī-niśītha-jāgaraṇe eva ārabdha-paripūrite uttararāmacaritasaṁjīvanākhya-ṭippaṇe.."

In these circumstances we need not be surprised if these performances do not reach a very high standard of excellence in the art of exposition—a characteristic that is a distinction of the Arthadyotanikā of Rāghavabhaṭṭa.

A commentator on a literary work of art is expected to help us to understand the work, to appreciate its full significance as well as its subtle charms and at the same time interpret the work in a manner, as far as possible closer to the poet. He is expected to give us a reliable text, note the variant readings and perhaps give us indications for his choice of a particular reading and rejection of another. If there are other interpretations offered then he is expected to help us to accept the best. A commentary worth the name must not in any case suffer from two faults, one of saying what should not be said 'avaktavya-ukti' and the other of not saying what ought to be said, 'vaktavya-tyāga'. Tripurāri rightly observes that 'vyākhyās' suffering from these faults are not regarded as good by the wise:

"santi yadyapi caitasya vyākhyāḥ prācyās tathāpi tāḥ /
avaktavyoktivaktavyatyāgābhyāṁ nādṛtā budhaiḥ' //"
(BP on MM.)

Judged in this light, a student of Rāghavabhaṭṭa's Arthadyotanikā easily finds that he does carry out his duties as a commentator in an almost ideal manner.

In the context of a Sanskrit text, the first question that always and invariably arrests our attention is the question of a full, flawless and a reliable text. In the case of the Abhijñānaśākuntala this problem is very interesting because of the additions and elaborations in point of scenes and verses. From his commentary it appears that Rāghavabhaṭṭa is not inclined to regard these additional verses or the celebrated Śṛṅgāric elaboration of the Third Act as genuine as he does not comment on them. But he is careful enough to give his observations regarding the variant readings that he had before him. One may draw attention to the places: I.2,13,17,18,21,27;II.6,9,10;III.7,8,12;IV.5,6,13;V.3 11,VII.8 : where he has noted or suggested an alternative reading. He notes such variants in the prose Sanskrit and Prākrit passages as well. Thus in 'ramyāḥ tapodhanānāṁ pratihatavighnāḥ kriyāḥ' (I.12) he explains 'ramyāḥ' and also explains the other reading 'dharmyāḥ' as 'vedabodhitācaraṇatvena ramyāḥ' and 'dharmādanapetā dharmyāḥ' and rightly accepts the first being more poetic. Attention could be drawn to his discussion at I.21 when he notes that 'karṇāntikacaraḥ' has an alternative reading in 'karṇe antikacaraḥ' and points out that the reading 'karṇāntikacaraḥ' carries with it the flaw of 'abhavanmatayoga'. Nor does this reading has any special merit in it that it suggests the close proximity of the bee. He justifies the singular in 'karṇe' as it is conducive to the development of the 'svabhāvokti' in the verse. At II.6, he points out that 'viśrāmam' in 'visrāmaṁ labhatām' is un-Pāṇinian. At II.9 he tells us that for the 'rūpoccayena manasā vidhinā kṛtā nu' an alternative reading is seen in 'rūpoccayena ghaṭitā manasā kṛtā nu' and he explains both these. In the latter he takes 'kṛtā' as 'dhyātā' and observes that Śakuntalā was first contemplated in the mind and then accordingly created by combining all beautiful things while in the first, the idea is that the Creator created Śakuntalā by a combination of all the beautiful things but he used his mind to create her and not his hands with the result that this creation has been exceedingly fine and delicate, brilliant with an especial lustre as no hands have fashioned her form. This way of reading the line and interpreting it makes it a fine compliment to the 'kānti' of Śakuntalā. At II.10 he notices the reading 'phalamapi ca' for 'phalamiva ca' in 'akhaṇḍam puṇyānām phalamiva ca tadrūpamanagham' and after having done full justice to the fine ideas in the verse remarks that, as it is, the 'alaṅkāra' in the verse is 'mālopamā' but the reading 'phalamapi ca', if accepted, would make it 'mālārūpaka'. At IV.6, in the celebrated 'pīḍyante gṛhiṇaḥ katham nu tanayāviśleṣaduḥkhairnavaiḥ' he notices the variant 'katham na' in place of 'katham nu' and adds significantly that this reading would require the use of 'kāku'. As an instance of a prose line where a variant has been noted, attention could be drawn to Act V, where Śakuntalā observes: 'aho kim me vāmetaram nayanam visphurati'. This has a variant in 'kiṁ me vāmam dakṣiṇam nayanam' and Rāghavabhaṭṭa explains 'vāmam pratīpam'.

At some places Rāghavabhaṭṭa has himself suggested new 'pāṭha's with a view to avoiding the poetical flaws in the lines of Kālidāsa. He in a sense practically rewrites the line and adds 'iti doṣaparihārārtham paṭhanīyam.' Thus while commenting on the exquisite I.18 'sarasijamanuviddham' etc. Rāghavabhaṭṭa points out that the second line' 'malinamapi himāṁśorlakṣma lakṣmīm tanoti' suffers from two faults 'kartṛprakramabhaṅga' and also a 'vākyaprakramabhaṅga'. The construction 'śaivalena' in the first line and 'valkalena' in the third line would for the sake of symmetry require the word' 'lakṣma' in the second line also in the instrumental (tṛtīyā), and this would have made the meaning very clear. As it is, the meaning so far as this second line is concerned is not immediately clear. To overcome all these difficulties he suggests that the second line should be read as 'śiśirakiraṇamālī sundaro lakṣmaṇāpi' (p.21). Similarly in the beautiful and lucid line of Kālidāsa at III.7. 'patrāṇāmiva śoṣaṇena marutā spṛṣṭā latā mādhavī' Rāghavabhaṭṭa thinks that there is 'prakramabhaṅga' so far as the placing of the word 'iva' is concerned and the word 'latā' also hangs about rather insignificantly and indeed is superfluous. He therefore suggests that the line be read as 'saṁspṛṣṭā dalaśoṣaṇena marutā sā mādhavīva priyā' / iti pāṭhe ivaprayogaprakramabhaṅgo latāśabdasyāvakratvam ca parihṛtaṁ bhavati). In a similar way to avoid the flaw of 'paryāyaprakramabhaṅga' he would at III.12 read the celebrated line 'śriyā durāpaḥ kathamīpsito bhavet' as 'kathaṁ na labhyeta naraḥ śriyārthitaḥ'. Rāghavabhaṭṭa would, to avoid 'prakramabhaṅga' read the line 'asyāmaham tvayi ca samprati vītacintaḥ' as 'tvayyatra cāhamiti samprati etc.' at IV.13..And thus at many other places we find Rāghavabhaṭṭa so to say 'correcting' the lines of the master. At these places, he reveals his critical insight, close acquaintance with canons of poetry and also his own keen poetic sense. One may not agree with him in all that he says at these places and 'accept' his 'improvements' over the lines of Kālidāsa, yet one will have to concede that he has a point to make, though it is to be remembered that he is judging Kālidāsa in the light of the canons of Sanskrit rhetorics which had assumed a rigidity in his own times. Kālidāsian lines are naturally flexible with happy turns and musical phrases and have in them a very clever placement of words quite in harmony with the emotion to be expressed and the peculiar disposition of the speaker concerned. But writing in an age when 'prakramabhaṅga' and 'avimṛṣṭavidheyāṁśa' and 'punarukti' were considered as serious faults, Rāghavabhaṭṭa tries to remove these irregularities in his own way.

To cover the ground of Raghavabhaṭṭa's critical observations—a part of which is already covered in foregoing paragraphs with a view to giving a complete idea, one has to note the following: At I.12 Rāghavabhaṭṭa would suggest 'svasmin pratyeti no cetaḥ' in place of the very familiar 'ātmani apratyayaṁ cetaḥ' for his reading removes the faults of 'arthapunarukti and avimṛṣtavidheyāṁśatva' that are present in the accepted reading. At I.13 he notes that in 'ramyāḥ tapodhanānām pratihatavighnāḥ kriyāḥ' the word 'ramyāḥ' has an alternative in 'dharmyāḥ' and explains both these words as 'veda-bodhita-ācaraṇatvena ramyatvam' and 'dharmāt anapetāḥ dharmyāḥ' respectively. He has done well in choosing poetic 'ramyāḥ' in preference to the prosaic 'dharmyāḥ, a fact to be seen in that he comments on the former word first. At I.17 in the line 'dhruvam sa nīlotpalapatradhārayā śamīlatām chettum ṛṣiḥ vyavasyati' Rāghavabhaṭṭa's reading 'samillatām' is definitely superior to 'śamīlatām' and is therefore to be accepted. Since he observes 'kvacit śamīlatām pāṭhaḥ' he is to be taken as noting it and also not accepting it since he mentions it later. In the first place 'samit' would be 'ucita' in the case of a 'ṛṣi' and would form a part of the daily activities of the sage. It, however, could be said in favour of 'śamī' that we get 'agnigarbhāṁ śamīm' in IV.4 where Kālidāsa speaks of the Śamī tree as a feminine symbol for Śakuntalā and secondly, the 'samits' are made of this tree. It is to be conceded that in both, the point to be conveyed is, as he points out, 'atyanta-asambhavanīyatva and atikāṭhinya' in the action of the sage and in the 'upameya' respectively. While commenting on the exquisite I.18 Rāghavabhaṭṭa points out that the line 'malinam api himāṁśoḥ lakṣma lakṣmīm tanoti' though beautiful does not agree well both with the line that preceeds and with the one that follows it. In 'sarasijamanuviddham śaivalenāpi ramyam' and 'iyam adhikamanojñā valkalenāpi tanvī' there is a certain symmetry which is violated in the second line. He is seen observing: 'vākyatrayam padakadambakātmakam dvitīyam tu kriyā-kārakānvitetyetadrūpam'. And further, here the Upamāna is not the agent, hence the order suffers. Thus there are both the flaws of Vākyaprakramabhaṅga and the Kartṛprakramabhaṅga. Thirdly in 'lakṣmīm tanoti' it is the 'sāmānyadharma' that appears to be presented to us and so the intended meaning does not readily come to the mind. He therefore suggests, as has been already pointed out, an alternative line, to be read as 'śiśira-kiraṇamālī sundaro lakṣmaṇāpi' in place of our too familiar 'malinamapi himāṁśoḥ lakṣma lakṣmīm tanoti'. The faults pointed out by Rāghavabhaṭṭa may all be there yet one does not feel like agreeing with him for the Kālidāsian line has the quality of a certain balance as in 'dāma laṅghitam bhramaraiḥ' while the alternative 'śiśirakiraṇamālī' though a paraphrase of 'himāṁśu' is all a liquid phrase like the 'lola-ali-kalila-mālā' as described by Daṇḍin while discussing the different styles in his Kāvyādarśa I. It has been already pointed out, that at I.21 Rāghavabhaṭṭa would prefer 'karṇe antikacaraḥ' to 'karṇāntikacaraḥ' for this latter reading is suffering from the flaw of 'abhavanmatayoga'. At I.27 Rāghavabhaṭṭa suggests 'adyāpi stanavepathośca janakaḥ śvāsaḥ pramāṇādhikaḥ' in place of the familiar 'adyāpi stanavepathum janayati śvāsaḥ pramāṇādhikaḥ' –if one were not to be satisfied with this reading inasmuch as it has no adjective agreeing with the word 'śvāsaḥ. At II.6 in the line 'viśrāmam labhatām etc'. the word 'viśrāmam' being an un-Pāṇinian form, deserves to be replaced by the word 'viśrāntim' according to Rāghavabhaṭṭa. At II. 9 Rāghavabhaṭṭa points out that the line' rūpoccayena manasā vidhinā kṛtā nu' has a variant in 'rūpoccayena ghaṭitā manasā kṛtā nu' but appears to prefer the first since he explains it at good length and brings out its full significance by observing that the creator did not use his hands in shaping Śakuntalā, for in her case, the mass of beauty in the three worlds, 'tribhuvanavartirūpasamudāya', was the material cause, the Upādānakāraṇa, while the mind was the instrument, the sense, for creative activity, Karaṇa. At II.20 he points out that 'phalamapi ca' in place of 'phalamiva ca' in the celebrated 'akhandam puṇyānām phalamiva ca tadrūpam anagham' changes the figure of speech, a Mālopamā into a Mālārūpaka. At III. 7 one is not inclined to disregard the familiar 'na tu grīṣmasya evam subhagam aparāddham yuvatiṣu' in favour of the alternative suggested 'nidāghasyaitādṛgyuvatiṣu na tāpastu subhagaḥ' though this latter seeks to get over the difficulty in the use of the genetive, as Rāghavabhaṭṭa says, 'asmin pāṭhe ṣaṣṭhīdoṣopi parihṛtaḥ'. In a similar manner perhaps our age-old partiality for what we suppose to be Kālidāsian would make us reject as unnecessary and therefore uncalled for, the attempt of our commentator to practically re-write the verse 'kṣāmakṣāmakapolamānanamuraḥ' etc. In an effort to remove the flaws of 'prakramabhaṅga, arthapunarukti' and 'iva-prayogaprakramabhaṅga' Rāghavabhaṭṭa proposes to read as follows: 'vaktram kṣāmakapolayugbhṛṣamuraḥ' for'kṣāmakṣāmakapolamānanamuraḥ';'klāntataraṁ' sayugmamadhikaṁ namraṁ cchaviḥ' for klāntataraḥ prakāmavinatāvaṁsau cchaviḥ pāṇḍurā; and finally 'saṁspṛṣṭā dalaśoṣaṇena marutā sā mādhavīva priyā' 'for patrāṇāmiva śoṣaṇena marutā spṛṣṭā latā mādhavī' at III.8. Again at III.12, one finds it difficult to be convinced that the familiar line 'śriyā durāpaḥ katham īpsitaḥ bhavet' has its beauty marred by a glaring 'paryāyaprakramabhaṅga' and therefore does deserve to be corrected as 'katham na labhyeta naraḥ śriyārthitaḥ'. Rāghavabhaṭṭa notices that for Śakuntalā's expression, after III. 20, 'Porava, rakkha vinaam (avinaam) maanasantattavi na hu attano pahavami' there is an alternative in' maanavahiaao vi kannaaao attano na ppahavanti' and that this reading introduces the figure of speech, the Aprastutapraśaṁsā. It need not be stated in so many words that one is likely to prefer here, as Rāghavabhaṭṭa himself has done, the simple, more direct earlier expression. In IV. 5, in the line 'anyebhyaḥ vanadevatākaratalaiḥ āparvabhāgotthitaiḥ' Rāghavabhaṭṭa notices a 'kartṛprakramabhaṅga' and therefore suggests 'anyaiḥ taiḥ' for 'anyebhyaḥ' At IV.6. in the much too familiar 'kaṇṭhaḥ stambhitabāṣpavṛttikaluṣaścintājaḍam darśanam' the phrase 'cintājaḍam darśanam' makes the line suffer from the flaw of 'uddeśyapratinirdeśya-prakramabhaṅga' according to our commentator and therefore he suggests in its place 'dṛṣṭiḥ jaḍā cintayā' to remove the flaw. In the last line of this verse he notices that the words 'katham nu tanayā' have an alternative in 'katham na tanayā' and adds that this latter would require a 'kāku' to convey the meaning. In IV. 13 also, in the line 'asyām ahaṁ tvayi ca saṁprati vītacintaḥ' is noted by Rāghavabhaṭṭa the flaw of 'kramaprakramabhaṅga'. and an alternative is suggested by him as 'tvayyatra cāhamiti samprati vītacintaḥ'. But as Rāghavabhaṭṭa has himself pointed out this 'pūrvanirdeśa' of the Navamālikā is indeed significant, for it must have made Śakuntalā very happy —'śakuntalāparigṛhītā seti tasyāḥ santoṣotpādanārtham asyāti pūrvanirdeśaḥ, tena kramaprakramabhaṅgaḥ parihṛto bhavati.' And hence this 'pūrvanirdeśa' is to be preferred on strong psychological grounds to the alternative proposed even though this latter introduces the figure of speech Yathāsaṅkhya. At V.3, Rāghavabhaṭṭa suggests 'vṛddhasya viklavagateḥ' for 'prasthānaviklavagateḥ' to remove the flaw of 'arthapunarukti' and at V. 11, he suggests almost a re-writing of the whole verse as 'snātaḥ abhyaktamiva śucirasucimiva prabuddhaḥ suptamiva svairagatiḥ saṁyatamiva', a mode which introduces the proper order in the familiar 'abhyaktamiva snātaḥ śucirasucimiva prabuddha iva suptam' and—'baddhamiva svairagatiḥ' since this latter suffers from two 'prakramabhaṅgas'. At VII. 8, he thinks that the line 'santānaiḥ tanubhāvanṣṭasalilā vyaktim bhajanti āpagāḥ' suffers from the flaw of 'aprayuktatva' in the phrase 'santānaiḥ' and 'avācakatva' in 'naṣṭa' and therefore suggests an improvement. as 'kārśyenākalitāmbhasaḥ pṛthutayā vyaktim bhajanty āpagāḥ' Lastly, Rāghavabhaṭṭa notes that the words of Śakuntalā in reply to the question from Sarvadamana about Duṣyanta, which are given as 'vatsa te bhāgadheyāni pṛccha' have also a variant as 'vatsa te bhāgadheyāni' a mode that at once introduces the figure of speech Rūpaka and along with a world of emotion and feeling. It is difficult to choose, for 'vatsa te bhāgadheyāni pṛccha' is equally Śakuntalā-like, a lady who has come to feel the power of 'bhāgadheya' with all her experiences.

All this discussion will indicate how Rāghavabhaṭṭa has been a very good critical student of the text he is commenting upon and how he has been very careful to note the variants, the pāṭhas, and to explain their significance as well. One may not agree with him everytime he picks up the flaw of 'arthapunarukti', or of 'avimṛṣṭavidheyāṁśa' or of 'prakramabhaṅga' in the lines of Kālidāsa, yet to understand him properly one has to well remember that an age did appear in Sanskrit Poetics which in its rather inordinate love for order and symmetry became almost blind to the graceful twists and turns that literary expression takes, it being essentially a creation of a human mind. Poetry when it seeks to express an emotion as well as storms and stresses felt by the human mind cannot, in the very nature of things be expected to conform to the principles of mathematical and mechanical order and symmetry. Poetry is indeed a strange world in which these very violations become significant and beautiful while the order and symmetry become or tend to become monotonous and dry. It is to be noticed that Rāghavabhaṭṭa has also taken care to note other interpretations which he often introduces with 'anye vyācakṣate'—a fact that is an indication of the care he took when he set himself to the task of writing his commentary on this great work, the Abhijñānaśākuntala.

Nothing of importance and significance misses his critical eye. A close student of Poetics, he knows that words like the verb 'vam', to vomit, are not to be used in poetry but he rightly points out that there is, as a matter of fact, nothing 'aślīla' in the line 'sparśānukūlā iva sūryakāntāḥ tadanyatejobhibhavāt vamanti'at II.7. He remarks 'atra vamanti iti aślīlaśaṅkā na kāryā / yatra svavācye vāntaśabdaḥ prayujyate tatra doṣaḥ' and refers to Daṇḍin. His discussion regarding the use of 'antareṇa' in 'atha bhavantam antareṇa kīdṛśaḥ tasyāḥ dṛṣṭirāgaḥ' is illuminating and he reveals his acute scholarship in trying to maintain that here we have the accusative for the locative; 'saptamyarthe dvitīyā'. He notes the distinction between 'antarā', and 'antareṇa', notices the various meanings and uses, especially in the sense of 'without and between', then he notices the use of the word 'antareṇa' by Kālidāsa himself in the Mālavikāgnimitra, refers to the relevant Sūtra, the Vṛttikāra too and also gives a positive instance to support his view in 'vijjujjoam marai rattim' and after all this discussion, concludes that 'the view that 'bhavantam' is accusative is wrong-'atrāntareṇa tatrabhavantam iti dvitīyā iti tu yat sa bhrama eva'. This is a good and complete philological note, one has to concede. He has been equally clever and alert in detecting the subtle scheme of 'chekavṛttyanuprāsas' in which Kālidāsa revels in many of his verses. Reading such comments of Rāghavabhaṭṭa is a sheer pleasure. One may refer here to one instance by way of an illustration. II. 2 is a superb composition by Kālidāsa and the verse runs as:—

> 'snigdham vīkṣitam anyato'pi nayane yat preṣayantyā tayā
> yātam yacca nitambayoḥ gurutayā mandam vilāsād iva /
> mā gā ity uparuddhayā yadapi sā sāsūyam uktā sakhī
> sarvam tat kila matparāyaṇamaho kāmī svatām paśyati' //
> II. 2

Without appearing anywhere either artificial or deliberate Kālidāsa has indulged in a very liberal use of letters n, t, s, y, and m's and this has materially contributed to the music of the lines. The words having a clever scheme of alliteration simply glide on. Rāghavabhaṭṭa is quick to notice the figures of speech as well as the clever arrangement and choice of words. He remarks:

> "madhyakārakadīpakālaṅkāraḥ / hetusvabhāvoktiś ca / nayaneyeti yantyāyātam iti tayātayeti chekānuprāsaḥ / nayaneyeti yatoyaditi yātaṁyeti tasyaivaikavācakānupraveśalakṣaṇaḥ saṅkaraḥ / sa eva vṛttyanuprāsenāpi pūrvārdhe / uttarārdhe tu vṛttyanuprāsaḥ' /"

And this is what Rāghavabhaṭṭa does at almost every significant place. In this manner he offers us considerable help in understanding the music and the subtle schemes underlying the choice of words in the verses of Kālidāsa. It would be no exaggeration to say that no other commentator is seen paying so much attention and so consistently to this very significant aspect of the verses, the metres and the words employed, as Rāghavabhaṭṭa does.

Kālidāsa is great in every department and so the musical lines and the simple dialogue have often to convey something deeper. Rāghavabhaṭṭa offers us considerable help in understanding the thought of Kālidāsa by making the intended meaning absolutely clear. Kālidāsa 'rarely expresses and invariably suggests', therefore, Rāghavabhṭṭa's help is indeed most welcome. He takes care in pointing out the 'arthāntarasaṅkramitavācya' even in the cases of very simple words and one may in this context refer to a few illustrations. At I. 20 in 'yad āryam asyām abhilāṣi me manaḥ' Rāghavabhaṭṭa explains the word 'āryam' as 'āryam śreṣṭham me mama jitendriyasya puruvaṁśa-utpannasya duṣyantasya iti arthāntarasaṅkramitavācyam'. He points out that in 'mamāpi kaśyapasutām anusmṛtya mṛgayāviklavam cetaḥ' the word 'kaśyapasutā' has been deliberately used to convey the noble and high birth of Śakuntalā/'kaśyapasutām śakuntalām/ anena kim api ābhijātyam dhvanayati/'. When the 'bhramara' hovers about the 'vadana' of Śakuntalā, Rāghavabhaṭṭa does not fail to add significantly 'anena padminītvam uktam asyāḥ'. When in the Third Act Śakuntalā prevents Duṣyanta from kissing her, 'Śakuntalā pariharati nāṭyena' Rāghavabhaṭṭa adds 'anena mugdha-vyavahāro'pi uktaḥ'. In the celebrated line 'anāviddham ratnam madhu navam anāsvāditarasam' II. 10, some as our commentator notes, understand 'madhu' as 'madya'. Rāghavabhaṭṭa rightly points out how this view is wrong and in the process reveals himself to be a real 'rasika'. He observes, 'kecana madhuśabdena madyam vyācakṣate/tat asat/tatra navam iti viśeṣaṇam viruddham syāt, jīrṇasya eva tasya uttamatvāt/tathā ca- 'jinnasurā sahina'iti/asau eva 'raghau-purāṇasīdhum navapāṭalaṁ ca'iti/. Who will not nod in assent to whatever Rāghavabhaṭṭa is saying here? Rāghavabhaṭṭa reveals himself indeed to be a poet when he comments on the exquisite 'darbhāṅkureṇa caraṇaḥ kṣata iti akāṇḍe'. II. 12. He points out that the word used is 'darbhāṅkura' and not 'darbha' for otherwise there would be no 'vyāja', pretence in the ruse resorted to by Śakuntalā. He observes 'darbhāṅkureṇa caranaḥ ksataḥ iti/na tu darbheṇa/tasya sattve vyājo na syāt/ aṅkurasya adṛsyamānatayā vyājasambhavāt/ato aṅkurapadena vyājena vilambitam iti dhvanitam'. At many places Rāghavabhaṭṭa has made the dhvani absolutely clear and his commentary is indeed an 'arthadyotanikā'.

But perhaps Rāghavabhaṭṭa is at his brilliant best when he offers explanations of Kālidāsa's lines and words and proceeds to make the poet's ideas quite clear, especially when it could be said that he seeks to expand the ideas of Kālidāsa. Thus when Kālidāsa, with his high aristocratic artistic sense that was always reluctant to waste words, would say about the beauty of Śakuntalā simply 'yauvanam aṅgeṣu sannaddham', we find Rāghavabhaṭṭa expanding the idea and explaining these words of the master in the manner of a worthy poet, for he remarks:

> 'atra aṅgeṣu iti bahuvacanena vadane kāntimattā nayanayoḥ taralatā kaṇṭhe kambutrirekhāvattvam vakṣasi stanojjṛmbhaṇam nābhau gambhīratā nitambe madhyanimnatvam ubhayabhāge caturasratvam jaghanajaṅ-

ghājānumaṇḍalorudeśānām māṁsalatvam gatau savilāsatvam ityādi dhvanitam'.

What Kālidāsa implies, Rāghavabhaṭṭa explains, what Kālidāsa suggests, Rāghavabhaṭṭa expresses. He does not miss any detail whatsoever. One may refer to another illustration. Repentant Duṣyanta is chiding the ring, the aṅgulīyaka; 'katham nu tam bandhurakomalāṅgulim karam vihāyāsi nimagnam ambhasi'. VI. 13. Rāghavabhaṭṭa proceeds to explain Kālidāsian 'tam' as 'tam raktotpalacchavim atimṛdulam mayā vāraṁvāram svahṛdayanyastam/yena atiprītyā tava dhāraṇam kṛtam tam/'. This is what one expects a commentator precisely to do. One can in this very context refer to his comments on I. 3; II. 10; III. 18; V. 20 and so on. Rāghavabhaṭṭa often adds his own similes and adjectives to make the meaning clear and in the process makes the whole more charming. Thus at VI. 10 to explain Duṣyanta's 'asannivṛttyai tadatītamete manorathā nāma taṭaprapātāḥ' Rāghavabhaṭṭa observes,'..nāma iti alīke / alīkamanoratha ityarthaḥ / te taṭaprapātā iti bhinnarūpakam / yathā varṣāsamaye gaṅgādeḥ taṭa oghena pīḍyamāna ahamahamikayā patanti/ ekaḥ patati tadupari anyaduparitaraḥ/evam manorathānām eke vilīyante anye utpadyante te api vilīyante taditare utpadyante ityarthaḥ'/.

Rāghavabhaṭṭa's attempt to read the famous love-letter written by Śakuntalā to her royal lover, indeed, should secure for him a pretty safe niche in the annals of Sanskrit poets and poetical literature. The temptation to quote him in full so as to give a proper idea of his masterly performance is very difficult to resist. Śakuntalā writes:

> 'tava na jāne hṛdayam mama punaḥ kāmo divā'pi rātrāvapi /
>
> nirghṛṇa tapati balīyaḥ tvayi vṛttamanorathāni aṅgāni' // III. 14.

Rāghavabhaṭṭa explains: 'nirghṛṇa niṣkṛpa tapayatyadhikam tvayi vṛttamanorathāni iti hetutvena yojyam / aṅgānīti bahuvacanena mārdavātiśayaḥ dhvanyate / tava hṛdayam iti viśeṣopādānāt svasyotkaṇṭhātiśayataḥ tasya tadabhāvo dhvanyate / arthāpattyalaṅkāraḥ / atha ca hṛdayam manasorasoḥ iti viśvaḥ / tena tava hṛdayam gopurakapāṭāyamanam ripudanujanivahaśaraśataiḥ api abhedyam / evambhūtam aham na jāne / api tu jāne āptajanavacanāt / ata eva me aṅgāni sarvāṇi divāpi rātrāvapi tāpayati kāmaḥ / tava tu vakṣomātramapi na tāpayitum śaktaḥ / yadi tāpayet tadā nirghṛṇa nirjugupsa nidāghasamayaśītalataramatkucaparirambhaṇāya āgaccheḥ / ghṛṇā jugupsākṛpayoḥ' iti viśvaḥ / tādṛśam tava vakṣa āliṅgitum icchāmi iti abhilāṣoktiḥ / anumānālaṅkāraḥ / atha ca tvayi viṣaye vṛttaḥ 'jātaḥ' manorathaḥ yeṣam tāni / āliṅganam bhujayoḥ manorathaḥ tvatkāntijharapravāhapānam tu cakṣuṣoḥ tvadvacanāmṛtasarasi nimajjanam śravaṇayoḥ tvanmukhasarojaśvāsaghrāṇam nāsaḥ śaśāṅkakomalatvadaṅkārohaṇam nitambasya tvatkaratalamelanam kucayoḥ ityādi / evambhūtamanorathāni mama aṅgāni kāmaḥ adhikam tāpayati / tvam tvevam niṣkṛpaḥ yatsvabhaktānyapi pareṇa tāpyamānānyapi sahase tat tava hṛdayam aham na jāne kṣatrahṛdayam iti na jāne / paraiḥ pīḍyamānam kṣatriyaḥ paritrāyate svabhaktam tu sutarām iti upālambhaḥ / mama punaḥ madīyam hṛdayam na jāne / tat tu tvayi vartate / tadabhāvāt hṛdayaśūnyā aham varte iti bhāvaḥ / kevalam tadeva tvayi gatam iti na / api tu kāmo abhilāṣo'pi tvayi viṣaye dine rātrāvadhikam tapati vardhate lakṣaṇayā / 'kāmaḥ smare abhilāṣe ca'iti viśvaḥ / iti anunayoktiḥ / tena madīyam bāhyamābhyantaram na kiṁcidapi matsambaddham iti śīghram āgaccha iti bhāvaḥ / śleṣānuprāsau / kvacit 'rattim pi'iti pāṭhaḥ / tadā rātrimapi iti arthaḥ / 'kālādhvanoratyantasaṁyoge dvitīyā'. This passage needs no comments and speaks for itself. Judged by all and any standards, this gloss must be reckoned as a brilliant piece of the art of exposition and the celebrated love-letter of Śakuntalā could not have received any better and more eloquent interpreter. One does realize after reading Rāghavabhaṭṭa as to how much one would have missed altogether in the appreciation of this exquisite piece of poetry from the immortal forest-maid of Kālidāsa. This passage is, one might say, typically representative of Rāghavabhaṭṭa's art of exposition, for here he expands the suggestions of the original before him, adds poetry to the discussion by his style, tries to lay before all that is implied, suggested or taken for granted, notes the variants, explains the grammatical points and fully squeezes even a simple significant phrase. It would be difficult to find a parallel to such an art of interpretation from amongst the other commentators and it could be safely asserted that Rāghavabhaṭṭa can successfully stand comparison with the best in this art even from the West.

Besides being a poet of a superior order Rāghavabhaṭṭa is a close student of dramaturgy. He has taken especial care to point out the five Avasthās, the different Arthaprakṛtis and the five Sandhis with all their sixty-four Sandhyaṅgas. Rāghavabhaṭṭa's analysis of the play from the point of view of the Sandhi and the Sandhyaṅga theory is fairly correct though it must be remembered in this context that a difference of views regarding the actual locations of the different Sandhyaṅgas is only to be taken for granted. Rāghavabhaṭṭa appears to accept the view of Udbhaṭa that the Sandhyaṅgas are restricted to the particular Sandhi to which they are said to belong. Of the sixtyfour Sandhyaṅgas Rāghavabhaṭṭa pointed out as many as fiftysix. He is also seen taking care to point out the different 'avasthā's of the hero and the heroine, which reveal to us the development of their love. An 'avasthā' stage is a significant psychological phase of the mind and therefore through the avasthās, an emotion is always developed, as manifested. Thus in the case of Duṣyanta have been pointed out Rati (p.16) Prītyatiśaya (p.16) Vismaya (18) Rateḥ sthāyitvam (34) Abhilāṣa (42) Cintā (46) Anusmṛti (46) Udvega (65) Anurāga (75) Mūrcchanā (169). In the case of Śakuntalā have been pointed out the Bhāva (28) Hāva (29) Helā (29) Śṛṅgāra-lajjā (32) Vilāsa (37) Lajjā (40) Abhilāṣā-kathana and Trapānāśa (72). Kālidāsa has revealed his rare skill in making all things in the play appear as natural as well as gradually developing towards culmination through these stages. Rāghavabhaṭṭa as he locates these stages enables the reader to appreciate the psychological development in the play.

Rāghavabhaṭṭa has also made an effort to locate the

various Nāṭyālaṅkāra and the Bhūṣaṇas in the play. Thus amongst the Nāṭyālaṅkāras he notices the Ullekha (14) Nīti (17) Mādhurya (21) Upadeśa (34) Āśiḥ (100) Akṣamā (135) and Praharṣa (196). From amongst the Bhūṣaṇas he notices the Prasiddhi (18) Nirukta (22) Anuvṛtti (30) Udāharaṇa (30) Nidarśana (32) Dṛṣṭa (36) Dākṣiṇya (48) Mālā (81) Upadiṣṭa (82) Manoratha (84) Saṁśaya (128) Hetu (160) Anunaya (195) and Madhura (200). He notices a few Sandhyantaras also. All these are dramatic embellishments which undoubtedly add to the literary qualities of the play, make the story move and at the same time reveal the character. Another significant fact is that while pointing out all these excellences Rāghavabhaṭṭa has taken a due notice of what authorities like Ānandavardhana, Bhoja, Mātṛgupta have to say about these matters. Rasa is the soul of the drama and Rāghavabhaṭṭa points out everywhere the 'rasa' that is being developed. Thus while commenting on the 'grīvābhaṅgābhirāmam I.7' he remarks

> 'atra bhayānako raso vyaṅgyaḥ/tasya mṛgagatam bhayaṁ sthāyibhāvaḥ/duṣyantādhiṣṭhitasyandanālokanamālambanavibhāvaḥ / tadanupātanaśarapātanautsukyādīnyuddīpanavibhāvaḥ/grīvābhaṅgārthabhakṣitatṛṇaskhalanaśuṣkoṣṭhakaṇṭhatvamukhavaivarṇyaśarīrasaṅkocaścancalādayo' nubhāvāḥ / trāsaśramaśaṅkā vegādayo vyabhicāriṇaḥ / kampādayāḥ sāttvikāḥ / etai raso vyajyate' /

This way of understanding the beautiful verses from the play not only reveals the cleverness of the commentator but it gives a glimpse into the great art of Kālidāsa himself where every word is deliberately used, a detail significantly added to arouse the desired emotion. At the end of the great Fourth Act Rāghavabhaṭṭa adds 'kaṇvapraveśānantarametadantena karuṇo raso dhvanitaḥ'. In a similar manner he points out the Śṛṅgāra, Adbhuta and the like. Perhaps in this context the most important is the essay on the rasa-analysis of the play with which Rāghavabhaṭṭa has rounded off his commentary.

All this discussion will show what immense and valuable help does Rāghavabhaṭṭa offer to us for a proper and deeper understanding as well as appreciation of the Abhijñānaśākuntala. As the commentary reveals its author Rāghavabhaṭṭa is more a poet than a mere commentator. His scholarship did not come in the way of his appreciation of poetry and it cannot be gainsaid that he has made full use of his knowledge of dramaturgy, poetics, grammar while writing his Arthadyotanikā. His is not a vain boast when he describes himself as 'niśātamati' and 'nāṭyālaṅkṛti śāstratattvavit.' Rāghavabhaṭṭa closes his commentary with a very fine verse :

'nāṭyālaṅkṛtiśāstratattvaviduṣā' abhijñānaśākuntala-
vyākhyeyam sarasā niśātamatinā śrīrāghaveṇa sphuṭā /
arthadyotanikābhidhā dhvanitadarthālaṅkriyānirbharā
śrīviśveśvarapaṭṭane viracitā tadbhaktiyuktātmanā //

One is bound to wholeheartedly endorse his view that his commentary possesses the four aspects of sarasā, sphuṭā, arthadyotanikā and at the same time dhvanitadarthālaṅkriyānirbharā'. How keenly one wishes that there were many more arthadyotanikās of this variety and that Rāghavabhaṭṭa's lead was followed by other Sanskrit commentators who came after him !!

IV. THE SAÑJĪVANA

(Ghanaśyāma on the Uttararāmacarita of Bhavabhūti)

To turn to Ghanaśyāma, after Rāghavabhaṭṭa and Pūrṇasarasvatī is to turn to a different spirit altogether. For the scholarship in the case of the two commentators Rāghavabhaṭṭa and Pūrṇasarasvatī was pleasingly softened by the poetry of the former and by the philosophy of the latter. But to Ghanaśyāma, scholarship brought nothing but high conceit and the natural result is that the commentaries proceeding from such a conceited spirit do not compare favourably with the commentaries produced by the spirits who strove to understand the great works of art and approached them with a certain sense of humility. They wanted to appreciate and not judge or criticise assuming an attitude of superiority. Ghanaśyāma on the other hand invariably felt that he was 'obliging' the author on whose work he was commenting.

Ghanaśyāma is a much communicative commentator so far as information about himself is concerned and to judge from this account that he often furnishes in the opening verses as well as in the closing portions of his commentaries, his attainments and achievements in the different fields appear to be really commendable. Wielding political authority and state responsibilities as he did, it is a pleasant surprise to find him devoting time to the writing of so many commentaries and feats in literary art. He wrote so many commentaries as well as original works but neither his religious zeal nor his literary persuits made him lose his haughtiness which perhaps his political distinction and his scholarship had inculcated in him. He informs us that he was a 'poet of poets', kavīnām kaviḥ' and also a 'Kośāvalivallabha' titles which undoubtedly richly he deserves, but in spite of all these qualities his performances as a commentator do not come up to our expectations. The feeling that one is likely to gather is that he cannot enter the spirit of the work he is commenting upon and that with his scholarship he is more trying to judge a work than attempting to interpret it to us. Considering the fact that Ghanaśyāma wrote his commentaries towards the evening of his life, having devoted his earlier age for creative activity, one is led to expect of him greater maturity as a critic in his commentaries. But an erudite person who thinks that he is 'obliging' a poet by condescending to write a commentary on his work, could not be, in the very nature of things, in a position to do better. Typical of his attitude are his verses with which he is seen opening his 'Prāṇapratiṣṭhā', a commentary on the 'Viddhaśālabhañjikā' of Rājaśekhara. Ghanaśyāma observes :

> 'naiṣārtho na kaveḥ idam matamaho kasyāpi nārtho bhavat yāste śṛṅgamamuṣya kiṁ nviti haṭhāt nerṣyām dharadhvam budhāḥ /
> mad-vākyam-anavekṣya vāḥ 'atra na gatiḥ tannandatām manmatau
> āho nindata rājaśekhara-kavau astūpakāro mama //
> 7. Prāṇapratiśṭhā

While telling us something about the mode of his commenting he does let go the opportunity of hitting out at the other commentators. He observes :

> 'sarve'pi vākyaṁ kaṭhinam vihāya vyākurvate yat sulabham tadeva /
> vayam tu dūre sulabham tyajanto vyākurmahe yat kaṭhinam tadatra //
> 15 ibid.

His attitude towards poets in general and the contempt and allofness that he often appears to hold, is perhaps best reflected in the following passage from his commentary 'Sañjīvana' on the Uttararāmacarita of Bhavabhūti. While commenting on the celebrated verse of Bhavabhūti 'yam brahmāṇam iyam devī vāgvaśyevānuvartate' I.2. Ghanaśyāma observes :

> 'atra punaḥ 'uttare rāmacarite bhavabhūtirviśiṣyate' iti vikramārkavacanaviśvāsinaḥ kecidalaṅkāravidyārthinaḥ vadanti / tat na viśeṣajñahṛdayaṅgamam / yataḥ 'kan-

iṣṭhikādhiṣṭhitakālidāsā' iti, 'ghaṭānām nirmātuḥ' iti, 'jānīte jayadeva eva', 'jānīte nitarām asau,' 'yohi, (Dhoyi) kavikṣmāpatiḥ' iti, 'daṇḍinaḥ padalālityam bhāraveḥ arthagauravam upamā kālidāsasya māghe santi trayo guṇāḥ'/ 'ko dhanañjayaḥ' iti, 'sūktiḥ sudhāsyandinī' ityādibhiḥ gīrbhiḥ ātmastuti-paranindā-varṣakal ākalāpinaḥ sarva eva kavayaḥ garvanidhayaḥ amīṣu ke...niraṁkuṣā ete tūṣṇīṁśīlaiḥ sāsmitāvinayābhinandanīyagavigumphāḥ' / (p. 5)

All this writing appears as interesting when one remembers that Ghanaśyāma himself was a poet and did describe himself as 'baddhāñjalyakhilaprayogasamayaḥ kośāvalīvallabhaḥ ghanaśyāmaḥ kavīnām kaviḥ,' in the introductory verses of this very commentary.

It is often said that Bhavabhūti writes dramatic poems and not dramas. One is led to believe that Ghanaśyāma had some such idea in his mind. He appears to raise this very interesting question in his commentary thus :

'nanu tadetat nāṭakameva na bhavati śṛṅgāravīrayoḥ anyatarasya rasasya prādhānyamiti niyamāt, karuṇarasasyaiva bhūyastvāt iti cet, satyam/śṛṅgāravīrānyatarasya aṅgitvam, anyeṣām aṅgatvena praveśo yadyapi, tathāpi, 'pradhānam yo, vamukhyatā/anye tvaṅgāni śṛṅgāra-vīrau tu prāyikau kvacit/,iti rūpakadāso—nāṭakamityevamagrāhyamālaṅkārikaiḥ'. (p. 5)

The argument seems to be that the Karuṇarasa, dominant as it is here, in the Uttararāmacarita, is likely to give more scope for poetry but less for action, yet the composition is to be regarded as a nāṭaka, for even the other rasas like the Śṛṅgāra and the Vīra do find some place, though a subordinate and contributory one. This certainly reveals his wider and sympathetic outlook towards poets, their experiments and the interrelation between the different rasas in a composition.

Yet with all this wider outlook, it appears that Ghanaśyāma could not appreciate himself and therefore could not interpret and elucidate to us the fine verses as well as the delicate touches by the great Bhavabhūti in this, his unquestionably superb play. His comments at these places clearly reveal that he himself had missed much in his reading and the appreciation of this piece. One may refer by way of proving this point to a few places. Thus at I.24 where Rāma tenderly remarks 'ayi katham vismaryate/alasalalitamugdhānyadhvasampātakhedāt. . tvamurasi mama kṛtvā yatra nidrāmavāptā/' after having looked with keen emotion and longing at the 'Śyāma vāta'—for Bhavabhūti has deliberately given before no utterance to Rāma but merely 'saspṛham avalokayati' when Lakṣmaṇa refers to the tree—Ghanaśyāma has nothing to add but a prosaic 'tasmāt itaravismaraṇe' pi nedam vismaryate iti bhāvaḥ'. At I.27 also after the fine 'aviditagatayāmā rātrireva vyaraṁsīt' he is no doubt clever in pointing out that in the verse 'kimapi' is 'anirvācyam yathā tathā'; aviralitau is 'mitho nīrandhrīkṛtau' and 'akrameṇa' is 'madanāveśapāravaśyāt pūrvottarasambandhabhāvena ityarthaḥ' yet his laconic remark after 'rātrireva vyaraṁsīt' that 'na tu saṁlāpaikadeśo' pīti bhāvaḥ' leaves one dissatisfied with its inadequacy in spite of his correctness. Or again at I.19 after 'mātṛbhiḥ cintyamānānām te hi no divasāḥ gatāḥ' he has to note simply 'pālyamānānām iti pāṭhaḥ sādhu'. The very choice of the reading here reveals the man. In Bhavabhūti 'cintyamānānām' to be replaced by pālyamānānām' !! One loves to imagine how Rāghavabhaṭṭa would have waxed eloquent over all these places ! It is not that Ghanaśyāma is not correct in his laconic remarks at these places but after a reading of the commentaries like those of Rāghavabhaṭṭa, Pūrṇasarasvatī and Vīrarāghava one does expect something more, at least from one who regards himself a poet of poets. Attention could be drawn to I.28 where the intense grief of Rāma is described in 'api grāvā roditi api dalati vajrasya hṛdayam'. Here Ghanaśyāma definitely spoils the effect by adding a prosaic 'ata eva grāvā śailopi roditi pratidhvanivyājena iti ūhyam'. Is really 'pratidhvanivyājena' necessary and what is its effect? At I.49 Rāma weeps ' roditi' after saying 'devi devi ayam paścimaste rāmaśirasā pādapaṅkajasparśaḥ' after what may be regarded as a very significant action given in 'Sītāyāḥ pādau śirasi kṛtvā'. But here too Ghanaśyāma has to observe 'rodityādikam aślīlam nāṭakāprayojyamapi' sarvam ca bhakṣyam kulam' ityādivat upekṣaṇīyam'! One could be excused for ascribing sheer insensitiveness to Ghanaśyāma. At III.14 Rāma, as a result of the 'sparśa' of Sītā says :

'prasāda iva mūrtaste sparśaḥ snehārdraśītalaḥ /
adyāpi ānandayati mām tvam punaḥ kvāsi nandini //

One feels that Bhavabhūti could not have thought of a better word for addressing, sambodhana, for Sītā, than the one that he uses here, 'nandinī' a happy word which is in a sense prompted by the word 'ānandayati' in the verse itself. Rāma has referred to 'ānandana' in an earlier expression 'ānandanena jaḍatām punarātanoti' and Sītā also hearing these words is made to observe'..ānandaniṣyandinaḥ āryaputrasya ullāpāḥ'. Bhavabhūti is trying to convey this 'ānanda' aspect and its emotional intensity felt so keenly by Rāma but Ghanaśyāma has to observe :

'nandini iti kaveḥ acāturyam / tathāpi nandayatīti dhātubalād avāntarabhedaḥ ūhyaḥ / nandinī prathamaikavacanam / nandinī tvam punaḥ kvāsi ityarthaḥ / punaḥ śabdaḥ vākyālaṅkāre / nandini iti sambodhanam iti kecit / tanna / devīti sambodhanasyaiva prābalyāt' (p. 60).

Bhavabhūti, the great poet that he is, begins the verse with the sambodhana 'devi' and rightly ends the verse on an intimate personal note in the sambodhana 'nandini'. These are, one often feels, the finer nuances of Bhavabhūti. It is the artistic and the psychological urge that determines the number and nature of the 'sambodhana's in such context and not the considerations of grammar and syntax. But perhaps the best instance how Ghanaśyāma goes astray altogether and spoils the effect intended by the poet can be seen in his comments on the too familiar III.17. In a very memorable verse Bhavabhūti describes the child as

'antaḥkaraṇatattvasya dampatyoḥ snehasaṁśrayāt /
ānandagranthirekovamapatyamiti badhyate' //

and on this very eloquent verse Ghanaśyāma has to say;

'ānandasya granthiḥ bījam tasya rekaḥ recanam tadeva apatyam iti arthaḥ / tathā ca dampatyoḥ antaḥkaraṇapremapūrvakasambhogaskhalitaḥ ānandarasaḥ eva apatyam iti bhāvaḥ'.

It is true that the Upaniṣads use the word 'ānanda' in the context of the 'upastha' but it is obvious that the entire sublimity of the original has been destroyed in the explanation by bringing it down to a sensual level. Bhavabhūti is all the while speaking of 'sneha, saṁśleṣaṇa, antaḥkaraṇatattva and ānandagranthi while the commentator is speaking in terms of 'suratātmaka upagūhana, taruṇastrīpuruṣa, bīja and recana'. The 'dampatī' of Bhavabhūti according to Ghanaśyāma is nothing more than 'taruṇastrīpuruṣa'. A yet another place that can be referred to in this context is VI.37 where Rāma is referring to an intimate experience of his, that has been called forth in his memory by the reference to the 'śilāpaṭṭa' round which the Kesara showered its flowers. Bhavabhūti is very subtle here. He makes Lava recite 'Rāma's words addressed to Sītā:—sītādevīmuddiśya raghupateḥ ślokāḥ' :

"tvadarthamiva vinyastaḥ śilāpaṭṭo'yamagrataḥ /
yasyāyamabhitaḥ puṣpaiḥ pravṛṣṭa iva kesaraḥ" //

Rāma has a world of emotions awakened in him—salajjasmitasnehakaruṇam—and refers to 'tat—samayaviśrambhātiprasaṅga', follows the vision that imagination conjures up, describes it in 'śramāmbuśiśirībhāvāt' etc., and then stays petrified—stambhita iva—. The vision is beautifully described in

"śramāmbuśiśirībhavatprasṛtamandamandākinī-
maruttaralitālakākulalalāṭacandradyuti/
akuṅkumakalaṅkitojjvalakapolamutprekṣyate
nirābharaṇasundaraśravaṇapāśamugdham mukham //"

There should be as a matter of fact no difficulty in concluding that this verse describes the vision that straightway comes from the 'viśrambhātiprasaṅga's connected with the 'śilāpaṭṭa' and the one that petrifies him now. Ghanaśyāma is certainly right in understanding the 'atiprasaṅga's as the sport of love and also right in explaining the different emotions in Rāma namely lajjā, smita, sneha and karuṇa but it appears that he has missed the significance of the verse in question altogether. He is again right when he remarks that what is conveyed is the exquisite natural beauty of Sītā, 'tathā ca nirupādhikam sītā-saundaryam iti bhāvaḥ'. But then what is the context of this description ? When was this beauty seen ? Ghanaśyāma's remarks appear somewhat confusing. He introduces the discussion of the verse with 'tadeva āha' apparently connecting the verse with the verse with the 'atiprasaṅga'. But later, he is seen observing that this description of Sītā without her ornaments refers to her bath, since the ear-ornaments are not there. His words are 'anena snānāvasara iti bodhyam'. What a poor understanding of a very delicate situation ! It is no wonder therefore that he interprets simply 'śramajalaiḥ śītəlībhavan' Bhavabhuti's 'śramāmbuśiśirībhavat' which Vīrarāghava does rightly explain as 'suratakālajasvedasalilena śītalībhavat'. Ghanaśyāma has missed so much and has yet the audacity to remark about other commentators that 'akuṅkumeti nirābharaṇeti ca dhvanī / evamādiṣu ghaṭṭeṣu paramanadhīnārthāḥ sudhīhitāścalamatayaḥ coravatpalāyantetarām avyutpannajaradbhittikhaṇḍāḥ, tadatra vyutpannā rasikā eva pramāṇam iti dik' / (p. 140)

This abusive and haughty use of language against other commentators is the habit of Ghanaśyāma, nay typical of him. Such language becomes all the more irritating because he does not enter into the examination of these other interpretations which he has in his mind when thus offering his high-handed condemnation. One may refer to his comments on III.47, the celebrated 'eko rasaḥ karuna eva nimittabhedāt etc'. Ghanaśyāma explains the idea as 'tathā ca āvartabudbudataraṅgādyupādhibhiḥ bhinnam sadapyambhaḥ vastutaḥ ekameva / tathā śṛṅgārādirasopādhiḥ bhinna iva dṛśyamāno'pi karuṇo rasaḥ anyatastadabhinnaḥ san ekə eveti bhāvaḥ' and then observes :

> 'asmin padye kecidārambhaśūrāḥ 'brahmāpi naram na rañjayati iti bhartṛharigirām pātrībhavantīti dik' /(p. 83)

without mentioning the view criticised and has not even cared to examine it. Again while commenting on the words of Sītā in the First Act where she describes Rāma as drawn in the picture as 'anādarakhaṇḍita-śaṅkara-śarāsanaḥ.' Ghanaśyāma is simply wild with rage and attacks those who read here a slighting reference to Śiva and observes 'khaṇḍitetyatra kecana śivadrohiṇaḥ pāṣaṇḍāḥ parihasanto dantān darśayanti, tat tuccham' and proceeds to point out how Rāma was a devotee of Śiva and had worshipped Lord Śiva for success in his undertaking. There are also passages which reveal him to be in sympathy with Vaiṣṇavism also for he regards Rāma as Viṣṇu. In the Third Act Rāma regains his consciousness and Sītā remarks 'pratyāgatamiva jīvitam trailokyasya' and on this Ghanaśyāma has to observe: 'etena rāmasya trailokyasya ca ekārthavarṇādadvaitameva prāmāṇikamiti kavinā siddhāntamārgo darśita iti bodhyam/ata eva 'harireva jagajjagadeva hariḥ' iti, 'sarvam viṣṇumayam jagat' iti, 'bhūtāni viṣṇurbhuvanāni viṣṇuḥ' iti prāñcaḥ'. (p. 57). Again at 'asanibandhanaṁ jātam jīvalokasya' with reference to the Hiraṇmayī pratikṛti in the Third Act he comments on 'jīvalokasya' as 'rāmasya iti arthaḥ / jīvaloka iti upalakṣaṇam/tathā ca jīvalokasya rāmasya ca abhedaḥ siddhaḥ/ata eva viśvam viṣṇuḥ iti / vāsanāt vāsudevasya iti paurāṇikāḥ./(p. 8) It would appear therefore that it is not his religious views that make him write strongly but it is habit to do so. Otherwise there was no necessity whatsoever of observing 'atra ghaṭṭārthe bahavaḥ prāṁśutarā strīprahartukāmā mūḍhā garvakharvatṛtīya vācyāyante iti dik' while commenting simply 'mameti hṛdayam jānāti iti arthaḥ' on Sītā's words 'aham etasya hṛdayam jānāmi mamāpyeṣaḥ' in the Third Act. (p. 59).

At times however he does make a point which deserves to be accepted. Thus in the Third Act, Rāma observes (p. 78) 'sarvathā sa evaiṣa bhagavānanekavāraparikalpanānirmito vipralambhaḥ punaḥ punaranubadhnāti mām' and here the word 'vipralambha' has been understood by some as 'vipralambha śṛṅgāra while by others it has been taken to mean 'viprayoga'. Ghanaṣyāma rightly takes it as 'vañcana' and while doing so, he is seen dismissing the other views disdainfully as in 'vipralambha śṛṅgāraviśeṣa iti kecit/ viprayoga iti anye / ubhe api śaśaśṛṅge' /. He also tries to connect this word 'vipralambha' with the word 'vipralabdha' used by Sītā and then quotes Amara to say 'vipralabdhastu vañcitaḥ'. We see him defending Bhavabhūti for separating 'ati' from 'śobhase' in 'kumāra ati hi nāma śobhase rathastha eva' in the Fifth Act. (p. 118). Ghanaśyāma rightly makes it clear that the use is for the sake of emphasis and observes 'atiśobhase iti vaktavyam iti pṛthakkathanam pramāda iti kaścit / tanna / 'atyantamaticaikāntamatyartham' iti śabdamālāyām svatantreṇābhidhānāt atīti pṛthak prayogo yujyate / hikāra uccāraṇapraudhye /. The word ati as the Śabdamālā indicates can be independently used.

All this discussion should make it clear that in Ghanaśyama we have a spirit that materially differs from that of Rāghavabhaṭṭa. He is at times very severe on Bhavabhūti also. At the end of the First Act Sītā is requested to mount the chariot and Bhavabhūti makes Sītā say :

> 'iam āruhāmi / (utthāya parikramya) phurai me gabbhabhāro saniam gacchamha' / (p. 30)

Ghanaśyāmā's comments on this situation and words are interesting. He observes that no lady would thus refer to her pregnancy in this manner in the presence of other men and the poet has indeed fared badly here, and he is guilty of gross impropriety. He observes : 'ittham puruṣa-samakṣam ṇissaṁkocatayā kathanam kaveḥ acāturyam / asmākam tu nirbhāti—'svagatam-phurai me gabbhabhāro/prakāśam-saniam gacchamo' iti pāṭhakramaḥ kalpanīyaḥ tāvadatra viśeṣajñāḥ pramāṇam iti' / (p. 30). In his own way he has given his view as to what ought to have been in place of what we find today in the text. Attention could be drawn to another similar place where Ghanaśyāma finds fault with Bhavabhūti. In the Third Act Vāsantī refers to the 'latāgṛha' III.37 where Rāma had to wait for Sītā who tarried being detained by the swans arousing her curiosity and affection. Vāsanti observes :

'āyāntyā paridurmanāyitamiva tvām vīkṣya baddhastayā
kātaryādaravindakuḍ malanibho mugdhaḥ praṇāmāñjaliḥ'

Ghanaśyāma takes objection to the 'añjali' here and observes that this is not how ladies from noble families behave. It becomes rather the courtezans than a lady like Sītā. He remarks 'añjaliriti kathanam kaveḥ acāturyam/veśyājanakriyamāṇo'yam vilāsaḥ na tu kulāṅganānām sampradāyaḥ'/ kadācidaparādhe sati satyaḥ pādapīḍanamevāracayantitarām, ityuccaihśirasaḥ/ alaukikavaidikaghaṇṭāpathamanthaviśeṣajñāḥ pramāṇam'/ (p. 74). Ghanaśyāma is dissatisfied with Bhavabhūti for his use of 'tasyāḥ' in III. 40

'sa evāyam tasyāstuhinanikaraupamyasubhago
mayā labdhaḥ pāṇirlalitalavalīkandalanibhaḥ'

and remarks 'atra tasyā iti kathane ubhayatra cāritārthyāt punastaditareti kathanam kaveḥ acāturyarūpakaḥ pramādaḥ'. It is obvious that he is considering here the reading 'taditarakaraupamya' for 'tuhinanikaraupamya' in the first line. Time and again he is seen speaking of the 'pramāda and acāturya' of the poet Ghanaśyāma's spirit perhaps is best seen in his audacious remark : '..kaumāraprakaraṇam tadidam nāṭakagarbhanāṭakātmanā dvikoṭikam kavicamatkṛtam saṁvidhānarahasyanārikelam atulamatiśilātale sphoṭitavānaham/ śiṣyaśiśuranasūyāpraguṇaguṇamaṇigrahayālubhiḥ anugrāhya iti dik'. Ghanaśyāma himself wrote a commentary on the Abhijñānaśākuntala, since he repeatedly observes 'asmadvyākhyāta śākuntale' but unfortunately this commentary is as yet not before us but should it become available some day a comparative study of his commentary with that of Rāghavabhaṭṭa should be very revealing. In his commentaries available, there are remarks which are sufficient to indicate that he is in no mood to spare even Kālidāsa and he shows his scholarly generosity with which he excuses and pardons Kālidāsa. But even in the absence of the full text of that commentary of his on the Śākuntala we can form some impression. While cemmenting on the exquisite verse of Bhavabhūti, III. 11

āścyotanam nu haricandanapallavānām
niṣpīḍitendukarakandalajo nu sekaḥ /
ātaptajīvitapunaḥparitarpaṇoyam
sañjīvanauṣadhiraso nu hṛdi prasiktaḥ /

Ghanaśyāma rightly points out that Bhavabhūti is trying here to create magic and music by the liberal use of 'nu' modelling his verse on the one by Kālidāsa, 'svapno nu māyā nu matibhramo nu' which is Śākuntala VI.10. But Rāghavabhaṭṭa could read the 'utkaṇṭhā-atiśaya' in the verse before him and various 'vitarka's conveyed to him the 'atyanta-asambhavanīyadarśanīyatvam' and as a result his exposition is a very fine piece of sympathetic and imaginative appreciation and interpretation. But Ghanaśyāma is not at all able to perceive either the fine and ardent eloquence or the intensity of feelings so admirably conveyed by Bhavabhūti, in the verse before him. Ghanaśyāma generously 'suffers the repetition' for this is an inheritance from Kālidāsa. Ghanaśyāma remarks 'svapno nu māyā nu matibhramo nu' iti asmadvyākhyātaśākuntalaślokānukaraṇamiva etatpadyānukārayoḥ punaruktiḥ kṣantavyā/ (p. 58). No comment is indeed necessary on this approach and understanding ! Ghanaśyāma rarely discusses points of interest from the point of view of dramaturgy and poetics. He does care to point out the Sandhis, the Sandhyaṅgas, the Nāṭyabhūṣaṇas and the Alaṅkāras. In this respect Vīrarāghava offers better help. Ghanaśyāma appears to point out 'dhvani' in many places but his cryptic remarks are by no means clear and he does not care to elucidate them for us. To illustrate the point, attention is to be drawn to the remarks 'dhvaniḥ or iti dhvaniḥ' to be met with in the commentary almost in an irritating manner. Thus while commenting on Sītā's 'ete khalu tatkālakṛtagodāna etc.' he comments simply 'kālakṛteti, dhvaniḥ'. Again, while commenting on Rāma's 'ayamāgṛhītakamanīyakaṅkaṇa' etc. I.18, he observes 'ayam āgṛhīteti dhvaniḥ'. On the words of Lakṣmaṇa 'ayam āryo hanūmān' he remarks 'ayamārya iti dhvaniḥ'. In a similar manner his remarks 'upasthāya iti dhvaniḥ (22), dīrghapravāsa iti dhvaniḥ. (34), anurodhaḥ anuvartanam, śraddhā tvāsaktiḥ iti padamālā, dhvaniśca (38) madya rāmasya iti dhvaniḥ (47), aparam itarat, dhvaniśca (48), yasyām te iti dhvaniḥ (49), upādānam iti dhvaniḥ (61), karṇamūlāt śravasorādibhāgāt / dhvaniśca (62), anurudhyante anuvartante/yameti dhvaniḥ (65), aparamiti dhvaniḥ (68), jīviteśvaram bhartāram / dhvaniśca (75), amīṣāṁ dṛśyamānānām iti dhvaniḥ (102), kaleti dhvaniḥ (103), anuṣṭhānam kriyām iti ca dhvaniḥ (116) gatam iti dhvaniḥ (117), Sundastrī iti kannaḍeṣu dhvaniḥ (121), nipāta iti dhvaniḥ (122), santam saumyam, dhvaniśca (125), santo lava iti dhvaniḥ (125), upādānam yamau iti dhvaniḥ (130), āsanam gṛhāṇa / dhvaniśca (133), yameti dhvaniḥ (153), and sadṛśo me iti dhvaniḥ (155). It is very difficult to understand what exactly he had in his mind while making these cryptic remarks and he appears to have used the word 'dhvani' in a rather loose manner. It is not clear whether he means by the word, alliteration, pun or suggestion, for all these ideas come to us when we study all these places critically. The form 'vyajyate' for bringing out the intended meaning has been used only twice (15,57), and at places which indeed are quite commonplace. Rāghavabhaṭṭa and Pūrṇasarasvatī reveal their close study of the works of authorities like Ānandavardhana, Bhoja and others and take note of whatever they have to say about the work on which a commentary is being written. Ghanaśyāma, however, does not appear to take any note of the appreciations and criticisms of these authorities of the play on which he is commenting. Thus for instance, he has nothing to say about the celebrated 'iyam gehe lakṣmī' I.38. where Ratneśvara sees the alaṅkāra 'bhāvika' since here we have 'waves upon waves' of expression due to the rising emotion. 'Harṣādibhāvitacetasaḥ hi vīciprāyāḥ uktibhedāḥ prādurbhavanti, yaiḥ apratyūhameva bhāvaḥ abhivyajyate / yā bhāvataḥ vācaḥ kāvyarūpāyāḥ pravṛttiḥ saiva bhāvikam' / (SP.431). Bhoja regards the verses 'ahetuḥ pakṣapāto yaḥ' V.17 and 'akiñcidapi kurvāṇaḥ saukhyaiḥ VI. 5 as indicating the 'Abhimāna in Love' and in 'advaitam sukhaduḥkhayoḥ' I.39 he sees 'sthairya as well as preyaḥ' enhancing the appeal to emotion. He cites 'athedam rakṣobhiḥ' I.28 as an illustration of 'Śoka' and the verse 'virodho viśrāntaḥ' VI.11 as an instance for 'rasapraśamasaṅkara'. But Ghanaśyāma has to say nothing about these verses nor does he reveal any awareness of these notices of Bhavabhūti taken by the rhetoricians.

Yet in spite of this what may be called as gross poetic insensibility which Ghanaśyāma reveals, his commentaries have great interest and importance for us. He offers help for textual criticism for he notes the other readings, 'pāṭha's and often suggests that there were other interpretations offered of the passages before him. What is perhaps of greater importance is the fact that in his commentaries he refers to a very large number of works and authors and also offers material interesting from the point of view of linguistic studies. Language and Lexicons appear to be the fields of his special interest rather than dramaturgy and poetics. Thus here in this commentary he gives us the Deśī words : 'theraṇa (85) ekalia (102) uddaṇḍa (123) galagala (144). The Maharashtra words noticed by him are : 'hajari for caraṇa (5), bhāvuji for bhāva (5), dhaḍakī for raṇaraṇaka (19), vikārite for vidāryantaḥ (40) gajabala for mahāsarpa ajagara (43), pājhara for srotas (45), kandi for granthi (46), avukani for sakala (48), uarāchī gatha for sabandhanam hṛdayam (51), bharato for bhriyamāṇa (55), raya āvali for lavalī (62) akasmat for akasmāt (75), khara ca for khara (79), dāḍī for kurcā (86), karavata for krakaca (88), ekalī for ekākini (103), sahāṇa for nikaṣa, śāṇa (106), uddaṇḍa for bahula (123), gholato for valana and gives-gholanta as deśī (124), panhata for prasnava (133), calo-manda for śilāpaṭṭa (139), vājantrī for vāditra (143) raṇa for araṇya (145). In the Prāṇapratiṣṭhā, his commentary on the Viddhaśālabhañjikā of Rājaśekhara, he gives 'muruma for gaṇḍasya upari sphoṭikā (29), khidakī for khidakkia (37), kanaḍe for karṇāṭī (47), cokaka, parakora for colaka (56), telaṅga for triliṅga (73), taṇṭā for taṇṭā (87), bhānāvalī for bhramāvalī (121), paṭa for paṭṭaka (223), Hindola (50), The Deśī words that we come across are 'khiḍḍakkiya (37), pulla (42), vahiali (43), hindolika (51), tampara (53), ollam (55), bhamario (85), tenta (87), tahkka (92) duttoli (99), puttalia (106), pajharai (106), sippi (108), dhakkijja (108), sikkivi (108), khelavida (121), bhānavida, bhamavida

(121), vakkara (131) ojjharanti (158) veda (167), rincholi (168), callijjantu (175), tanijjantu (175), vahira (175), vahirillic (217). One is likely to feel that this is an interesting and important feature that distinguishes the commentaries of Ghanaśyāma from those of others. We also meet with many observations regarding Prakrit forms and formations and in these matters he begs to differ from Kālidāsa and Bhavabhūti and others. It has to be admitted therefore that his commentaries have an importance from a philological point of view.

Ghanaśyāma's commentaries are also important because of the fund of information that they give us about Sanskrit authors and works. This also is a distinguishing feature o his commentaries, for other commentators do not quote as profusely and as widely as he does. Thus for instance we find him in the commentary on the Uttararāmacarita with which we are here primarily concerned, quoting from the following authorities : Agastya, Abhidhana, Amara (3), Amaramāla (19), Amaraśeṣa (55), Āgamatantra (89), Īśvarakṛṣṇamiśra (68), Uttararāmāyaṇa (13), Ubhayarūpakośa (19), Ekākṣarakośa (64), Kapila (49), Kāmandaka (41) Kāvyacintāmaṇi (116), Kāvyadīpikā (77), Kuṅkumakavi (40), Kedāra (18), Keśava (4), Gāthāsaptaśatī (85), Govardhana (85), Gauḍapādācārya (82), Cakṣurūpa (89), Chāndogya Upaniṣad (33), Jaya (107), Trikāṇḍaśeṣa (54), Trirūpakośa (34), Daṇḍin (44), Dayālava (135), Dvirūpakośa (47), Dhanañjaya (115), Dhanvantari (133), Dharaṇi (78), Dhvanimañjarī (140), Nandārjuna (102), Nandī (73), Nānārthamañjarī (87), Nāmanidhāna (141), Nāmamālā (23), Nāmābhidhāna (41), Nāmārṇava (80), Nīlakaṇṭha (10), Padamālā (91), Padārthamālā (59), Padmamālā (59) Padminīprakaraṇa (59), Purāṇa (92), Prabhākaramiśra (84), Bāṇa (150), Bilhaṇa (121), Bodhāyana (70), Bhaṭṭikāvya (22), Bhartṛmīḍha (30), Bhartṛhari (44), Bhāratacampū (15), Bhāravi (39), Bhoja campu (4), Makuṭa (63), Maṇḍanamiśra (44), Mayasiddhānta (134), Mahānāṭaka (18), Mahābhārata (97), Mahimnastotra (4), Māṭhara (46), Mudrārākṣasa (69), Mūkakavi (109), Mṛtyuñjaya (84), Medinī (26), Yādava (34), Ratnakośa (51), Ratnamālā (114), Rabhasa (20),

Rāmāyaṇa (57), Rudra (4), Rūpakādarśa (88), Liṅgapurāṇa (61), Līlādhara (80), Lolamba (144), Varadanta (82), Vararuci (65), Vastunirṇaya (135), Vāmana (15), Vālmīki (3), Vikramārka (4), Vikramacarita (21), Veṇīsaṁhāra (135), Vedanighaṇṭu (9), Vaijayantī (50), Śabdamañjarī (10), Śabdārṇava (46), Śāśvata (55), Śivagītā (12), Śṛṅgāramañjarī (64), Śrīnātha (85), Śrīsūktabhāṣya (134), Śrīharṣa (42), Samayapaddhati (63), Samāsanighaṇṭu (94), Saṁsārāvarta (10), Sārvabhauma (94), Sāhityamaṇḍana (95), Hanūmat-nāṭaka (52), Haradatta (134), Halāyudha (7), Hārāvali (10), Hāsamiśra (3), Hemacandra (36) and Haimakośa. (35) This is a formidable list indeed and will serve to give an idea of the scholarship that has gone into the making of this commentary. It becomes a matter for still greater surprise when it is remembered that this commentary was written practically in 'no time' for Ghanaśyāma himself informs us : 'śrīrāmanavamīniśītha-jāgaraṇe eva ārabdhaparipūrite uttararāmacarita-sañjīvanākhya-ṭippaṇe'. His reading is indeed wide and his memory must have been as alert as to furnish him with everything that was necessary to complete the commentary from the beginning to the end in one night only.

Commentaries of Ghanaśyāma appear to have an importance of their own since through these very numerous references to persons and works he throws valuable light on literature and authors about whom we know very little or nothing. The quotations that he gives from works now extinct are extremely valuable inasmuch as they give us an idea about the work and its contents. Thus he quotes from the work of Māṭhara : 'anuvartate pratīkṣate iti māṭharaḥ /(9), styāyate upacīyate iti māṭharaḥ /(46), dalati sphuṭati iti māṭharaḥ / (71), ācāmati cūṣati iti māṭharaḥ/(85), dhinoti prīṇayati iti māṭharaḥ /(118), dalati dīryati iti māṭharaḥ / (141) and indicates that this work was a 'dhātupāṭha'. Or again he is seen quoting from the Kośa of Kedāra : vṛttam ācarita—atīta-padya-caritra-vartule iti kedāraḥ / (18), rahasyam tu mantre ca iti kedāraḥ (34), aho bho he kimayyaṅgamukhaḥ sambodhanārthakaḥ iti kedāraḥ (36), iva upamāyām ca alike iti kedāraḥ (44), sthagayati kuṇṭhayati iti kedāraḥ (74), parityāgaviyogāntaghaṭaḥ pravilayastu tāḥ iti kedāraḥ (80), nivṛttamāṁso nirmāṁso vṛttamāsastu māṁṣalaḥ iti kedāraḥ (87), bhayotpādanahetoryā pratimā sā vibhiṣikā iti kedāraḥ (106), vighaso bhojanaśeṣaḥ iti kedāraḥ (110), athāgastya-vasiṣṭhayoḥ maitrāvaruṇimaitrāvaraṇau iti kedāraḥ (118), sāmagryamapi sambhāraḥ iti kedāraḥ (124), śirombuvacaneṣu kam iti kedāraḥ (125), yathaiva vā va yadvacca yathā vā iti kedāraḥ (134), adhyāyassargaḥ iti kedāraḥ (137), niḥsāre ca khilībhūte jīrṇam śuṣke bhayāspade iti kedāraḥ (140), artho'rthanaviṣayayoḥ dhanakaraṇavastuṣu iti kedāraḥ (144), darśanakṣaṇa apatastathaivākarṇanakṣaṇaḥ iti kedāraḥ (148), and 'pari syāt paritorthe' pi iti kedāraḥ (157). In a similar manner we get about eighteen citations from the Kośa of Kapila and about eleven from the Kośa of Nandī. Ghānaś-yāma refers to a number of Kośas and his commentaries deserve to be thoroughly scanned from this point of view. In this particular respect no other commentator could be placed by the side of this 'kośāvalī-vallabha'.

Ghanaśyāma appears to supply us with interesting information about authors as well. This information should prove very important if it is corroborated from other sources. To illustrate : we are told that 'vipulam çakṣuṣi vistṛtam nitamb iti gauḍapādācāryāḥ' (82), The plural would go to indicate that the author quoted is a highly revered person, for in other cases, the conventional singular is used as iti kedāraḥ, kapilaḥ and so on. This naturally brings to our mind the figure of the great Vedāntin Gauḍapādācārya, the author of the Māṇḍūkyakārikās and also perhaps of the Bhāṣya on the Sāṅkhyakārikās. This particular quotation is not seen in either of these works and appears to hail from some thesaurus. We are left to wonder whether there is a third work associated with him and which is not before us. This solitary citation would obviously need further corroboration to enable us to proceed further in the matter, but it sets us thinking.

A reference in this context could be made to another striking fact. Ghanaśyāma quotes seven times from the works of Kālidāsa but gives the name of the author as Īśvarakṛṣṇa-miśra and Bhartṛmīḍha. Thus we get

1. 'ata eva gaṅgāprapātāntanirūḍhśaṣpam iti Īśvarakṛṣṇamiśraḥ (68)
2. 'śaityam hi yat sā prakṛtiḥ jalasya iti Īśvarakṛṣṇamiśraḥ (76)
3. 'tasmin viprakṛta kāle' iti Īśvarakṛṣṇamiśraḥ' (129)
4. 'atra dīrye iti kaveḥ pramādaḥ na vidīrye kaṭhināḥ khalu striyaḥ iti kumārasambhave Īśvarakṛṣṇamiśrasya iva dayanīyaḥ (141)
5. 'śaityaṁ hi yat sā prakṛtiḥ jalasya iti Bhartṛmīḍhaḥ (30)
6. 'śakyam aravindasurabhiḥ iti Bhartṛmīḍhaśca (3)
7. 'aniṣṭhitāntarāja iti Bhartṛmīḍhaprayogavat kṣantavyaḥ' (8)

It should be clear from these references that Ghanaśyāma regards Kālidāsa to have been Īśvarakṛṣṇa Bhartṛmīḍha. If in his Sañjīvana, the commentary on the Uttararāmacarita he quotes from Kālidāsa under these names, in his Prāṇapratiṣṭhā, the commentary on the Viddhaśālabhañjikā, he shows that he was aware of the fact that these are works of Kālidāsa. Thus we get in the Prāṇapratiṣṭhā :

1. 'śakyam aravindasurabhiḥ iti kālidāsasya (36)
2. 'gaṅgāprapātāntanirūḍhaśaṣpam iti kālidāsaprayogāt na asāmañjasam iti āhuḥ (73)
3. 'prakṛteṣu kvacitpuṁliṅgasya napuṁsaka-liṅgatvam ucyate/ata eva 'aharamanahiyaadi iti śākuntale kālidāsena uktam (192)

There is therefore no possibility of a mistake on the part of Ghanaśyāma. He knew that these works were written by Kālidāsa and yet he was giving the two names Īśvarakṛṣṇa and Bhartṛmīḍha. The commentary on the Uttararāmacarita was written by Ghanaśyāma after his commentary on the Viddhaśālabhañjikā as the references like 'asmad vyākhyātaviddhaśālabhañjikā..(12, 15, 16) would indicate. He wrote a commentary on the Abhijñānaśākuntala as well. If as Ghanaśyāma appears to tell us Kālidāsa's name was Īśvarakṛṣṇa Kālidāsa, then we get from him a very valuable information about the greatest of our poets. We are told by Svapneśvara that Īśvarakṛṣṇa Kālidāsa wrote the Sāṅkhyakārikās, 'īśvarakṛṣṇakālidāsena kṛtāḥ kārikāḥ'. We find scholars like Keith and Hiriyanna placing Īśvarakṛṣṇa and Kālidāsa in the Gupta period and making them contemporaries. Could these two indeed be identical? The idea has been further developed by this author in his 'Kālidāsa, His Art and Thought'. It is obvious that further corroborative evidence only will enable us to decide the matter but it is to be conceded that Ghanaśyāma has given us some food for thought.

Ghanaśyāma's commentaries may not appear as very interesting from the point of view of pure aesthetics and it is no use comparing him with Rāghavabhaṭṭa and Pūrṇasarasvatī. He does not appear to feel any warmth for anything and he does not enter into dramaturgical and also rhetorical discussions deliberately, since he tells us in the Prāṇapratiṣṭhā that he avoids these discussions for fear of making his commentaries unduly lengthy—'grantha-vistāra-bhayena na aṅgasandhyādi lakṣaṇam proktam' (18). Yet his importance from the point of view of history of Sanskrit literature, lexicography and language cannot be overestimated. This Kośāvalī—vallabha, the proud and haughty spirit that he was, has also a safe place among the galaxy of Sanskrit Commentators. Bhavabhūti's forlorn hope for a 'samānadharmā' was not to be fulfilled by him !!

V THE CAMATKĀRATARAṄGIṆĪ

(Kamalā and Sundarī on the Viddhaśālabhañjīkā of Rājaśekhara)

The choice of this commentary of Sundarī and Kamalā on the Saṭṭaka Viddhaśālabhañjikā of Rājaśekhara for a study here need not make one feel that the claims of other commentators like Vīrarāghava or Jagaddhara have been ignored. There are other commentators with very creditable performances no doubt, but Sundarī and Kamalā do deserve a special and separate treatment in a study like this which attempts to note and study some worthy performances from among commentaries on Sanskrit dramatic compositions for several reasons. In the first place being women commentators they deserve our admiration and in the second place, their very fine performance that the Camatkārataraṅgiṇī is, does entitle them to full compliments from us and hence there should be no hesitation on our part in giving these two ladies their well-deserved place by the side of their husband Ghanaśyāma, a place which both by law and merits is all their own. Sundarī and Kamalā evoke our admiration for their sound scholarship, poetical genius and powers of lucid expression as well as exposition. The Camatkārataraṅgiṇī, their joint commentary on the Viddhaśālabhañjikā must be put down as a memorable contribution to the Sanskrit commentary literature. Lastly, it will be seen that there is some point in studying a commentary on Nāṭikā, after having had a look at the commentaries on the Nāṭakas and the Prakaraṇa, just with a view to showing that all the different forms of Sanskrit drama were properly attended to by Sanskrit commentators.

Of the two, Sundarī was married to Ghanaśyāma first, when she was hardly in her teens and when Ghanaśyāma also was hardly twenty. At the age of thirty or so Ghanaśyāma married Kamalā who also according to the prevalent customs then must have been very young and in her teens. In their being wedded to Ghanaśyāma, as a matter of fact, Sundarī and

Kamalā were wedded to scholarship and poetry and it is no wonder that they themselves were inspired for a literary effort. It cannot be doubted that their inspiration was Ghanaśyāma himself for whom very naturally they have the highest regard which they have expressed in so many words in their commentary. They speak of him as 'śrīmān kavīnām kaviḥ, pumbhāvaikasarasvatī bhuvi Ghanaśyāmo vijejīyate' (CT. 18). In a very pleasing and polished manner they chide their co-wife 'su-kavitā' who does not abandon Ghanaśyāma any time and clinging to him does not give him any leisure to attend to them. They observe : while describing her boldness

> 'lajjā nau rahasi prakāśamapi hā nāthānanendum sukham/
> cumbantī na vilajjase sukavite dhanyā sapatnī hyasi' /
> (27 CT)

and

> 'śayyāyām nava-rambhayoriva mudā pārśva-dvaye' pyāvayoḥ
> satyostvam bhajate suvṛtta-pada-gīḥśayyārucim vallabhaḥ/
> nainam vṛddhatamāpi muñcasi kathamkāram param nātmavat
> tvam jānāsi navoḍhayoḥ sukavite nāste 'nukampā tava //
> (28 CT)

These fine verses should indicate in some measure their regard for the poetical powers of their husband as well as their own capacity to compose elegant verses. They boast of the fact that Ghanaśyāma could compose poetry any time, so was completely at his mercy the Muse, but other ordinary poets like Rājaśekhara had to wait for particular time and hour for their muse to be awakened. They go on : 'etena tri-granthakārasya rājaśekharasya prātareva kavanasphūrtiriti spaṣṭam / pañcaṣaṣṭi-prabandhīkaraṇa-dhurandharāṇām asmatsanāthānām nāthacaraṇānām tu ghaṭikānām ṣaṣṭirapi nibandhān nirmātum nālam ityanitara-sādhāraṇo 'yam viśeṣo vatsarasatayā vatsalādibhiḥ asūyārasikaih anugrāhyāḥ'/ (p 23) Sundarī and Kamalā came to love poetry and literature as is evident from the several quotations from the proverbial observations like 'sarvam vinaśyati vihāya kavitvam ekam kāyena sākam', 'sādhu vicāryamārya', 'kā vidyā kavitām vinā,' 'vidyāratnam sarasakavitā', 'sukavitā yadyasti rājyena kim', 'madhu-kṣīra-drākṣā-madhurimā-dhurīṇā bhaṇitayaḥ', 'kamanīyāḥ kavayitā' etc. (p. 17). They were inspired by Ghanaśyāma and we therefore need not be surprised to find them imitating him in many respects. Thus they share with him his supreme self-confidence and also the courage for criticising the recognised masters like Kālidāsa and Bhavabhūti. They also reveal independence of spirit and though one may not wholeheartedly agree with them in all that they say, yet it has got to be readily conceded that they appear to have some point when they indulge in grammatical discussions. Like Ghanaśyāma they too are in the habit of quoting constantly from many writers and in the process they reveal their wide knowledge of Sanskrit lexicographical literature, sound grasp of Sanskrit and Prakrit grammar and lastly their very fine command over Sanskrit language and thorough acquaintance with Sanskrit classical literature.

They seem undoubtedly to give a happy homely and a feminine graceful touch when they open their commentary meekly introducing themselves as 'daughters in law' thus :

'Ayi santo bhavatpāda-padma-rāgāvalī sakhī /
snuṣayoḥ āvayoḥ bhāle jīyāt-kuṅkuma-rekhayoḥ' //
(3 CT).

and also in 'snuṣābhyām vivṛtiḥ kṛtā'. 25 CT). But as soon as the commentary proper begins they put on the scholar's robes and move about majestically and comfortably too. Ghanaśyāma had already composed his own commentary on the Viddhaśālabhañjikā, the Prāṇapratiṣṭhā and this he followed by his commentary on the Uttararāmacarita, the Sañjīvana. Since Sundarī and Kamalā refer to Ghanaśyāma's commentary on the Uttararāmacarita in their 'tathā ca bhadram tasya sumānuṣasya itinātha-caraṇa-vyākhyāta-uttararāmacarite' (p. 18) it is clear that they had the Prāṇapratiṣṭhā before them when they wrote their commentary on the Viddhaśālabhañjikā, the Camatkārataraṅgiṇī. A comparative study of these two commentaries on the Viddhaśālabhañjikā, the

Prāṇapratiṣṭhā and the Camatkārataraṅgiṇī therefore should prove to be very interesting. Sundarī and Kamalā take care to write fuller comments and also to write in a more clear style than that of Ghanaśyāma. They, however, have his challenging spirit and haughtiness and in his manner point out the mistakes of the poet by observing 'kaveḥ pramādaḥ' and also like him appear to dismiss the other commentators with scant respect by observing 'asaṅgatam vadanti paṇḍitamanyāḥ kecid'. (p. 15). About their own powers of interpretation they observe in Ghanaśyāmian style

'padasya ekasya jalpāvaḥ pramāṇānāṁ śatam....
ko likhet kaḥ paṭhet ko'dah pāṭhayettadviramyate' //
(35 CT).

Dr. J.B. Chaudhury would read 'yadi' for the two missing syllables in the first line but I would prefer to read 'śatam' again so as to intensify the proud assertion. Like Ghanaśyāma they too think that in a sense they are obliging Rājaśekhara by writing a commentary on his work. Referring to the two commentaries, the Prāṇapratiṣṭhā by their husband and their own the Camatkārataraṅgiṇī, they observe

'pitṛbhyām kanyakevāsmadvyākhyābhyām yā pracāryate
eṣaitābhyām budhā dṛgbhyām śālabhañjī vilokyatām'//
(37 CT).

Whenever they want to give their approval for what they consider to be not quite correct and to be of the 'would do' type, like Ghanaśyāma they use the patronising phrase 'kṣantavyam or dayanīyaḥ.

Of greater interest is the fact that like true critical students of a literary work they seem to study influences and imitations. They have pointed out at several places the influence of Kālidāsa over Rājaśekhara. Thus at I. 21. 'svapnaḥ kimeṣa kimu saṁvidiyam tu sākṣāt, jñānam kimetadubhayātmakamanyadeva' of Rājaśekhara is modelled on Kālidāsa's celebrated 'Svapno nu māyā nu mati-bhramo nu' for they state in clear terms 'etat kathanam 'svapno nu māyā nu matibhramo nu' iti kālidāsa-kavana-cchāyānusaraṇam iti bodhyam.' (p. 34). On Rājaśekhara's 'syātsaṅkalpakṛtaścakāsti manasaḥ kasyaiṣa rekhā-kramaḥ' (I.39 b) they observe 'tadidam 'citte niveśya parikalpitasattvayogeti nāthacaraṇa-vyakhyāta-śākuntalacchāyānusaraṇam iti jñeyam'. (p. 63). Again at II. 4. 'candro jaḍaḥ kadali-kandamakandaśītam.. kim candrikām kvacidasitaruciḥ prasūte' they point out that the 'bhāva' here is that 'tathā caivam amanojña-vastu-paramparā-nirmāṇa-kṛtābhyāso vidhātā īdṛśa-manojñaika-vastu-nirmāṇe'pi katham pravīṇo bhavet' and finally remark 'tadetat 'asyāḥ sarga-vidhau'iti bhartṛmīḍha-kavana-cchāyā-nusaraṇam iti bodhyam'. (p. 90). In a similar manner while explaining III. 1. d. 'yena drasṭumaham kṣame daśa diśastadvaktra-mudrāṅkitāḥ' they observe that this idea is to be met with in Śrīharṣa in his Naiṣadha when we get 'daśa diśaḥ khalu tādṛgakalpayallipikarī nala-rūpaka-citritā, in IV.15 (evam kathanaṁ dasa diśaḥ khalu iti śrīharṣa-kavana-cchyā-nusārīti bodhyam / p. 123). They point out that Rājaśekhara's III. 19. d. 'vāhyākāra-parigraheṇa tu vayam tattva-tyajo vañcitāḥ' is an imitation of Kālidāsa's celebrated 'vayam tattvānveṣāt' etc. 'tadidam' vayam tattvānveṣādityādi Śākuntalacchāyānusaraṇamiti bodhyam' (p. 162). It does not escape their notice that the phrase 'vidura-vasudhā' of Rājaśekhara is modelled on Kālidāsa's 'vidura-bhūmi' in the Kumārasambhava I. 24. : 'vidurabhūmirityādi kālidāsa-kavanānusārīti bodhyam.' (p. 164). They think it worth-while to point out the similarity between Rājaśekhara's 'sā asmadvilocana-cakora-candrikā' and that of Jayadeva's 'candramā rocayatu locana-cakoram' etc. : vilocanetyullekhaḥ' candramā rocayatu locana-cakoramiti jayadevakṛta-murārirā-gāṣṭapadīcchāyānusāri / (p. 62) At the King's remark 'anamanuvartatā smartavyā vayam' (p. 72) they are reminded of Śrīharṣa's smaraṇiyāḥ samaye vayam vayaḥ' II. 62 since they observe 'smartavyā ityetat smaraṇīyāḥ iti srīharṣa-kavana-cchāyānusāri iti jñeyam'. Rightly do they point out that the King's 'kva punarasau asmat-nayanāmṛta-vartiḥ' has its counterpart in Bhavabhuti's familiar 'iyam amṛtavartiḥ nayanayoḥ' etc.

While commenting upon IV. 4. where occurs a reference to the drinking of 'vāruṇī' by ladies they show in clear terms their disapproval of the same. They observe that the 'vāruṇī-prasaṅga' though common in earlier literature yet should not be used by the modern poets. They observe :

> 'vāruṇī-prasaṅgastu śiṣṭa-parigṛhīto yugāntara-viṣaya abhiprāyikaḥ / ata eva 'rudra-viṣṇu-vidhīndrādyairmunibhirdevyanugrahe / darśanīyam sasitāmbu sampūjya madhu pīyate' // iti śaktisaṁhitāyām/' tamapāyayatā pānamambikāmiti kumārasambhave / 'rāmo'śoka-vane pānam sītayā sahitaḥ papau' iti uttara-rāmāyaṇe/' vāruṇīmāpibadacyutāgrajā' iti yādava-carite ca / Yat tu bhagavatpāda-kālidāsādibhiraṅgīkṛtam asminneva yuge tatra teṣām tejoviśeṣeṇa pratyavāyo na vidyate/Na idānintanairevam vidheyam iti śiṣṭācāra iti dik'/ (p. 188).

One would feel like agreeing with this mild rebuke.

Sundarī and Kamalā, however, do not seem to pay much attention to the discussion of the 'alaṅkāra's, the Sandhis and the Sandhyaṅgas, or the metres though occasionally they try to point out the suggestions and the inter-relations of incidents and expressions in the play. In this respect, so far as the dramaturgic and rhetorical study of the play is concerned, their commentary cannot be compared with the commentary of either Rāghavabhaṭṭa or of Vīrarāghava, for these writers take special care to point out all these details and often enter into interesting discussions.

As a matter of fact, however, the importance of this commentary seems to lie in the fact that it is in a considerable measure and in many respects a complimentary one to the commentaries of Ghanaśyāma. For Sundarī and Kamalā also quote from the same Kośas from which their husband quotes and thus it is possible for us to trace further and more citations from these works which are no longer before us. It is seen that Sundarī and Kamalā quote from the Māṭhara-kośa or Dhātu-pāṭha and from Kośas like the Kedāra, Nandī, Saṁsārāvarta and others. From this point of view, these commentaries can be read together and portions of the text of the now extinct works like those of Nandī or

Rabhasa can be recovered in some measure. From the Māṭhara-kośa we get the following : dhunoti dhunoti iti Māṭharaḥ (ii) pūrayati ācchādayati vyāpnoti sthagayati iti Māṭharaḥ (24) stute stauti iti Māṭharaḥ (12) leḍhi bhakṣayati iti Māṭharaḥ (74) apakrāmati apayāti gacchati iti Māṭharaḥ (87) mārṣṭi mārjayati iti Māṭharaḥ (109) tapati tāpayati iti Māṭharaḥ (156). From the work of Nandī hail the following : ākūtam agrahaveṣau iti Nandī (35) āvṛttyavasarauṣadheṣu varaḥ iti Nandī (58) vikaṭam hāsyam iti Nandī (99) puṁsi vātulo vātya-cakra-bhramanīlā iti Nandī (110) pracaṇḍo duḥsaha iti Nandī (159) bhṛśārthe samyag iti Nandī (169) hṛdayam mana iti Nandī. To these quotations from the work of Nandī could be added the eleven quotations from Nandī which we get in the Sañjīvana the commentary of Ghanaśyama on the Uttararāmacarita. (pp. 68, 73, 76, 98, 100, 104, 110, 127, 131, 134 and 149). In this manner these commentaries enable us to have some idea about works that are now not before us.

From a cultural point of view also the Camatkārataraṅgiṇi has an interest all its own. Sundarī and Kamalā both were from Mahārāshtra and it is therefore natural that they should refer to the things Maharashtrian, now and then. The words, proverbs and practices that are here referred to are : vasaṇa (13) maṇake (13) puttalī (15) phaṇata (16) madācī polī (22) māñjarī ḍoḷe (22) sāṅkhalī (24) modyā ca pahāṭe (24) caukhaṇḍī (25) āṅgamoḍyā deṇe (26) khāje (31) mora morī (36) kālave (39) baṭṭamogarā (40) masurā (42) kuralakesa (46) prākārāgrañcāri (48) rāya āvaḷi (48) gatagānī (42) caitra śuddha tṛtīyā durgādolādhirūḍha gaurīpūja (50) kāṇḍī (51) karaṇḍā, ḍabā (32) vovī (55) mahārāṣṭra-paridhāna-nīvīniveśa (57) ghara (60) kāṭhi (62) ṭevī (63) cālane (65) sphoḍa (65) kikalī (71) kuvaḍī (71) kātarī (87) sajā (91) dānta sīṇā (91) utphālatā (93) chatā, jāṭi (94) cāṇḍā, cāndalā, ṭikali (95) vāraṁvār (96) bhombarā (96) padara (97) gulaṇi (99) jāḍave (101) rākhaḍī (101) teṅkāyo celo u (104) dharāvarimi (104) gauri ruṣṭā cet saubhāgyam nāiṣyati iti maharāṣṭrāṇām ābhāṇakaḥ (104) camatkūn (105) vahaṭali (110) prasṛtipāśa (110) panhale (110) kankaṇī (113) saṇam bāce dore

(117) sāvalibāi gāṇe-gharaṭṭa-bhramaṇa-keli-gīteṣu sāvalībāi iti mahārāṣṭrāṅganā gāyanti (122) śāyī (123) pāṭā (123) vase (123) tutore (130) urasī vāmam pādam nidhāya iti mahārāṣṭreṣu ābhāṇakaḥ (131) gholasarīcī māla (132) argalam vinā saṁcarasi iti mahārāṣṭra-bhāṣāyām arthāntara-camatkāraḥ (133) vahilī (136) vinoda (137) kātagoli (138) roditu, mauktikāni galanti mahārāṣṭrīyaḥ ābhāṇakaḥ (139) kaṭile (142) jagha (144) dorā (144) toṇḍa (147) droṇe (150) nalīce tīra (153) gābhādre (155) Śalākālā, śalākha (156) karpūra-śalākānirmāṇam mahārāṣṭra-prasiddham (156) śarkara-pratimā, varṇamarma (varṇa-kālāpacaya-marma) mahārāṣṭrā jānanti (158) putalī (158) apāta (158) davaṇā (158) khāmba (160) lāla (161) śikhariṇi-mahārāṣṭra-bhāṣāyām madhura-padārtha-viśeṣa-abhidhāna (166) khiḍakī (175) khilī (175) bāhera (175) jase āle tase gele (177) goṣṭhī (180) vivāha-lagna (182) rāya-keḷī (185) bālā (185) gāra (186) jāyaphalam ce vṛkṣa (188) magaja (188) bahece kāṭha (189) kañcoḷi (190) coli (190) phirakī (190) vāḷā, kaṅgaṇī (191) bucaḍā (191) khambaitta, jhuna (191) khambaitta, jhuṇā (191) seṭī (199) tabaka (203) gaccāṇḍī (206) antaḥpaṭi (209) jamīna (212) kānaḍā aṅgamā (222) and vacī (222). It is perfectly natural that these daughters of Mahārashtra should have used so many words from their own language in their elucidation of a Sanskrit text. It is interesting to note that the words from Maharashtra as they have given betray the influence of the fact that Sundarī and Kamalā were residing at Tanjore.

The Camatkāra-taraṅgiṇī is complimentary to the works of Ghanaśyāma in yet another respect. Ghanasyama quotes from and refers to so many authors and in this respect Sundarī and Kamalā follow him. In the process they tell us some information about these authors from whom they quote. Among the works and authors referred to by Sundarī and Kamalā can be mentioned the following : Appayya Dīkṣita, (20) Varāhamihira Ācārya (74) Māgha (49, 129, 140) Mudrā-rākṣasa (92) Amara (10, 92, 144 etc.) Murāri (56, 192) Kṣemendra (142) Karpūra-mañjarī (143) Mayūra (27) Mahānāṭaka (35) Bhavabhūti (39, 38) Śrīharṣa (12, 90, 97, 123, 149 Jayadeva (55) Vararuci (160) Bhagavatpāda (11,

22, 24, 63 etc.) Kālidāsa nearly thirty times. These references only indicate how they were well-read and also show their critical attitude for they often point out the mistakes of these celebrities. Thus Murāri is criticised at p. 56 for his 'kokā-prīti-cakora-pāraṇa-paṭu-jyotiṣmatī locane; Amara and Kṣemendra at p. 142 for their 'tārāsthi-sañcaya etc; Kālidāsa and Bhavabhūti at p. 90 for their placements of words in the context of 'purāṇa' and 'nirmāṇa'; Śrīharṣa for his use of the word 'sodarī-nilaya' (p. 149) and so on. They criticise authors for their Prakrit forms also and one may refer to Bhāṣāmalla (148) Kālidāsa (147) and so on. There cannot be any doubt about the fact that their reading was both wide as well as critical.

Amongst all these references and quotations, those from Kālidāsa deserve our special attention. These references are very interesting as well as very important. These are as under:

1. 'tathā ca 'kuryām harasyāpi pinākapāṇeḥ dhairya-cyutim ke mama dhanvinaḥ anye' iti Bhartṛmīḍhaḥ' / (p. 11).
2. 'ata eva 'vayam tattvānveṣāt madhukara hatāstvam khalu kṛtī' iti nātha-caraṇa-vyākhyāta-śākuntale' / (p. 27).
3. 'etat kathanam 'svapno nu māyā nu matibhramo nu' iti kālidāsakavana-cchāyānusaraṇam iti bodhyam'/ (p. 34).
4. 'ata eva 'caturasra-śobhi vapuḥ vibhaktam nava-yauvanena' iti kālidāsaḥ'/ (p. 59).
5. 'tadidam 'citre niveśya parikalpita-sattva-yogā' iti nātha-caraṇa-vyākṛta-śākuntala-cchāyānusaraṇam iti jñeyam'/ (p. 63).
6. 'ullasitetyādikam 'unmīlita-bhrūlatām' iti nātha-caraṇa-vyākhyāta-śākuntala-cchāyānusāri iti jñeyam' / (p. 67).
7. 'ata eva 'unmīlitam tūlikayeva citram' ityādi Bhartṛmīḍhaḥ'/ (p. 68).
8. 'atra kaveḥ purāṇa-niramāṇa-śabdayoḥ madhyam

śabda-viśeṣasya kathanam kālidāsa-bhavabhūtyoḥ iva kṣantavyam'/ (p. 90)

9. 'yadyapi 'kadalī-viśeṣāt' iti kālidāsa-prayogāt kadalī-kandam iti kaveḥ pramādaḥ tathāpi aṇḍam vṛkṣa-mūle ca iti nāma-nidhānāt kadalikāyāḥ mūlabhāga iti samādheyam'/ (p. 90)

10. 'tadetat 'asyāḥ sargavidhau' iti Bhartṛmīḍha-kavana cchāyānu-saraṇam iti bodhyam'/ (p. 90)

11. 'atha sā kandukaiḥ...reme 'iti kālidāsa-vacanena strīṇāmapi khelane sampradāyāt krīḍanam pra-kramate'/ (p. 93).

12. 'atra pātotpāta iti asya unnata-vinata iti asya ca paraviruddhaḥ kaveḥ pramādaḥ 'carācara-sthāvara-jaṅgamānām' iti prayuktavataḥ īśvarakṛṣṇasya iva kṣantavyaḥ'/ (p. 96)

13. 'ata eva 'śakyam aravinda-surabhiḥ' iti, 'idam kavibhyaḥ, iti nātha-caraṇa-vyākhyāta-śākuntala-uttararāmacaritayoḥ'/ (p, 98)

14. 'khe khela-gāmi' iti kālidāsaḥ'/ (p. 108)

15. 'ata eva 'abhirūpa-bhuyiṣṭhā' iti nātha-caraṇa-vyākhyāta-śākuntale'/ (p. 115)

16. 'ata eva 'sthitaḥ kṣaṇam pakṣmasu tāḍitādharaḥ payodharotsedha-nipāta-cūrṇitaḥ, iti bhartṛmīḍhaḥ'/ (p. 128)

17. 'ata eva 'rajanī-timirāvaguṇṭhitetyādi' bhartṛmī-ḍhaḥ'/ (p. 141)

18. 'atra rathāṅga-nāmna iti vaktavye rathāṅga iti kathanam kaveḥ pramādaḥ 'rathāṅga-nāmaka' iti, 'rathāṅganāmnoriva' iti amarasiṁha-īśvarakṛṣṇami-śrābhyām abhidhānāt'/ (p. 144)

19. 'akkhareti kālidāsādīnāmiva kaveḥ pramādaḥ'/ (p. 147)

20. 'accariam iti kālidāsa-śrīharṣādīnāmiva kaveḥ pramādaḥ'/ (p. 156)

21. 'ata eva 'tapati tanugātri' iti nātha-caraṇa-vyā-khyātaśākuntale'/ (p. 157)

22. 'khane khane iti Kālidāsādīnāmiva kaveḥ pramādaḥ'/ (p. 158).

23. 'thambeti' kālidāsādīnāmiva kaveḥ pramādaḥ'/ (p. 160)
24. 'tadidam 'vayam tattvānveṣāt' ityādi śākuntalacchāyānusaraṇam'/ (p. 162).
25. 'viduretyullekho 'vidura-bhūmi' ityādi kālidāsakavanānusāri iti bodhyam'/ (p. 164).
26. 'ata eva 'saṅgatam śrīsarasvatyoḥ' iti bhartṛmīḍhaḥ'/ (p. 173).
27. 'muktā-kalāpasya ca nistalasya' iti īśvarakṛṣṇamiśraḥ'/ (175)
28. 'aparaḥ paścimaśca asau 'pūrvāparau' iti bhartṛmīḍhaḥ'/ (p. 178)
29. 'jamadua' iti Kālidāsādīnāmiva kaveḥ pramādaḥ'/ (p. 184)
30. 'rudra-viṣṇu-vidhīndrānyaiḥ munibhiḥ devyanugrahe/ darśanīyam sasitāmbu sampūjya madhu pīyate' iti śaktisaṁhitāyām/ 'tam apāyayatā pānam ambikām' iti Kumārasambhave/'rāmo'śokavane pānam sītayā sahitam papau iti Uttara-rāmāyaṇe/vāruṇīm apibat acyutā-graja iti Yādavacarite ca/yattu bhagavatpāda-kālidāsādibhiḥ aṅgīkṛtam asminneva yuge tatra teṣām tejoviśeṣeṇa pratyavāyo na vidyate/na idānintanaiḥ evam vidheyam iti śiṣṭācāraḥ iti dik'/ (pp. 187-188)
31. 'atra nayana-nipāta iti etat kaveḥ acāturyam 'sahasram akṣṇām yugapat papāta' iti, mama nayana-nipāta' iti kālidāsa-nīlakaṇṭhayoḥ prayogavat kṣantavyam'/ (p. 211)
32. 'vāmam prakoṣṭhe' rpita' iti kālidāsaḥ'/ (p. 216)
33. 'śrīmatripuryam iti avyastaḥ prayogaḥ 'sarva-śaiḷa' iti kālidāsasya iva kṣantavyaḥ'/ (p. 221)

Of these citations Nos. 1 (Bhartṛmīḍha), 4 (Kālidāsa), 7 (Bhartṛmīḍha), 11 (Kālidāsa), 16 (Bhartṛmīḍha), 17 (Bhartṛmidha), 25 (Kālidāsa), 27 (Īśvarakṛṣṇamiśra), 28 (Bhartṛmīḍha), 30 (Kalidāsa), 31 (Kālidāsa) and 33 (Kālidāsa) are all from the Kumārasambhava with the name of its author given in the bracket. This clearly indicates that according to Sundarī and Kamalā, the author of the poem Kumārasambhava was Īśvarakṛṣṇa Bhartṛmīḍha Kālidāsa.

Further citations Nos. 10 (Bhartṛmīḍha), 14 (Kālidāsa) and 26 (Bhartṛmīḍha) are from the Vikramorvaśīya and the author of the play is taken by Sundrī and Kamalā to be Bhartṛmīḍha Kālidāsa.

Again, citations Nos. 2, 3, 4, 6, 13, 15, 21, 24, and 32 are from the Abhijñāna-śākuntala and the author is given as Kālidāsa in citations Nos. 3 and 32. Elsewhere only the play is named and not its author.

Citations Nos. 12, 18 and 27 give the name of the author as Īśvarakṛṣṇa (12), and also as Īśvarakṛṣṇa miśra (18, 27); cita tions nos. 1 ,7, 10, 16, 17, 26, 28 give the name as Bhartṛmīḍha and citations nos. 3, 4, 8, 11, 14, 19, 20, 22, 23, 25, 29, 31, 32 and 33 give the name as Kālidāsa. The fact that Sundarī and Kamalā show their familiarity with the names of Kālidāsa as Īśvarakṛṣṇa Bhartṛmīḍha or Īśvarkṛṣṇamiśra and it would need indeed some very weighty considerations to make us reject this very clear testimony in favour of these names of tha poet Kālidāsa. It need not be supposed that it is rather unusual for Sanskrit commentators to quote from one and the same author giving his different names. Pāṇini, the great grammarian is often referred to as Pāṇini, Ācārya, Śālāturīya and Dakṣiputra. Similarly we find Patañjali being referred to as Patañjali, Gonardīya and Phaṇī. In the Camatkāra-taraṅgiṇī itself we find Sundarī and Kamalā quoting from Bhavabhūti giving his name Bhavabhūti as well as Śrīkaṇṭha. Thus we have :

1. 'roditi iti aślīlakathanam 'api grāvā roditi' iti kavayatām śrīkaṇṭhādīnāmiva nāṭaka-viruddhamālaṅkārikasambhavamapi kaveḥ acāturyam kṣantavyam' / (p.169)
2. 'bāṣpa-vārāṁ pravāhaḥ (III. 24) ullekho'yam 'ayam tāvad-bāṣpa' iti śrīkaṇṭha-kavana-cchāyānusāri iti bodhyam' / (p.170)

The name Bhavabhūti is also given (p. 90) and the Uttara-rāmacarita is also referred to without the mention of its author. (18, 98, 64). In a similar manner they refer to Amarasiṁha as merely Amara. We know that Bhavabhūti himself informs us that his name was Śrīkaṇṭha, in his celebrated 'śrīkaṇṭha-pada-lāñcchanaḥ'. It could therefore be regarded as very natural if Sundarī and Kamalā quote from Kālidāsa giving us his other names as were known to them. There is no valid reason for taking them to be in the wrong. In a few minds is likely to arise the question of the reliability of Sundarī and Kamalā and in this context, it can be stated this much : they have very freely and liberally quoted from Śrīharṣa, Murāri, Kṣemendra, Appayyā Dīkṣita, Vararuci, Jayadeva, Māgha, Bhavabhūti, Hanūmat, Śaṅkarācārya, Viśākhadatta, Amara but in all these places they were found to be correct and reliable. Obviously any verification becomes difficult when they quote from works like the Kośas, the Kedāra, Nandī, Acyuta or from the Dhātupāṭha of Māṭhara, since these works are not before us. But it can be asserted that so far as their references to known authors and works are concerned, it is not seen anywhere that they mislead us. It, therefore, becomes difficult for one to regard them as committing mistake when they refer to so famous an author like Kālidāsa or to regard them as committing mistakes in giving us the authors of celebrated works like the Kumārasaṁbhava, the Vikramorvaśīya and the Śākuntala.

It was in my 'Kālidāsa, His Art and Thought' that I had tried to put forth the view that Kālidāsa, the celebrated author of the Ṛtusaṁhāra, Mālavikāgnimitra, Kumārasambhava, Vikramorvaśīya, Raghuvaṁśā, Meghadūta and the Abhijñānaśākuntala, was in reality Īśvarakṛṣṇa Vindhyavāsa Bhartṛmīḍha and that he was the same as Īśvarakṛṣṇa, the author of the Sāṅkhyakārikās, the pearl of Indian philosophical poetry. At that time I had in my discussion mainly relied on the seven quotations from the commentary of Ghanaśyāma on the Uttararāmacarita of Bhavabhūti and on the remark of Svapneśvara that the Sāṅkhyakārikās were written by Īśvarakṛṣṇa Kālidāsa. Ghanaśyāma in the Sañjīvana, while quoting from the different works of Kālidāsa, clearly indicates that the name of the author of these works according to him is Īśvarakṛṣṇa Bhartṛmīḍha. It is too much to imagine that Ghanaśyāma has committed a mistake and has 'sinned seven times' in repeating the mistake, and that too in the case of an author like Kālidāsa and in the context of the works like the Raghuvaṁśa and the Śākuntala.

We now find Sundarī and Kamalā supporting Ghanaśyāma and it would be too much to say that the wives have simply blindly repeated 'the mistake of their lord'. It is true that Parkinson has only recently pointed out that in the academic world the second teacher teaches what the first has taught him and the first teaches whatever he likes and occurs to him. Sundarī and Kamalā therefore can be taken as simply repeating whatever Ghanaśyāma taught them. To such a view there is no reply and one has to patiently wait for further corroborative evidence. In this manner the commentary by Sundarī and Kamalā is complementary to the commentaries of Ghanaśyāma.

In its more restricted field, the Camatkāra-taraṅgiṇī is a supplement of the Prāṇa-pratiṣṭhā, the commentary of Ghanaśyāma on the Viddha-śālabhañjikā. In a sense, it is an improvement too. In some places they have given the view of Ghanaśyāma (p. 50, 185) but these are not to be found in the Prāṇapratiṣṭhā and the conclusion therefore is to be drawn that they must have consulted him while writing their commentary. They were fortunate in having Ghanaśyāma's commentary before them (p. 67, 219) and in having the benefit of actual discussion and consultation with him. Further, Ghanaśyāma writes in his usual laconic style and appears to pay little attention to the Sanskrit portion of the text while Sundarī and Kamalā take delight in elucidating these portions. They have, as is usual with the Sanskrit commentators, noted the variant readings of the text and they often give us good readings. Thus at I.11. they would prefer to read 'prācī-nīla-biḍāla-locana-rucām..'for 'prācī-bāla-biḍāla-locana-rucām' etc. (p. 22) and add that this is 'yuktaḥ pāṭhaḥ, atiprakāśakatvāt. At I.27 in 'ye dolā-keli-karā kimapi mṛgadṛśām..' they would prefer 'manasi' to 'kimapi' and add 'kimapi iti bhrānṭaḥ pāṭhaḥ, manasi iti supāṭhaḥ (p. 44) and thus at several places. The value of their commentary for a reconstruction of the text of the play therefore cannot be over-estimated.

The Camatkāra-taraṅgiṇī is indeed a 'River of Marvels'. It is undoubtedly a work of remarkable intrinsic merit and has a value all its own being a work by women commentators. Sundarī and Kamalā, the co-wives collaborate here and produce this commentary. The wives, as is evident, have been inspired by the husband, for whom very naturally their admiration is very great. One has nothing but admiration for these two young daughters of Maharashtra residing at Tanjore who learnt Sanskrit and Prakrit at the feet of their husband, became good scholars of Sanskrit and Prakrit Grammar, read widely Sanskrit literature and tried with success their hands both at poetry and the art of interpretation. What a cultured family Ghanaśyama's must have been ! One cannot help feeling that Sundarī and Kamalā could not have named more happily their joint work, the Camatkāra-taraṅgiṇī'.

VI THE DIṄMĀTRADARŚINĪ

(Nārāyaṇa-bhaṭṭa-śiṣya on the Bhagavadajjukīyam of Bodhāyana)

To turn to the Diṅmātradarśinī on the Bhagavadajjukīya is to turn to a commentary on a Prahasana, a popular form of the Sanskrit drama. So far, we had a glance at the commentaries on the Nāṭakas, the Abhijñānaśākuntala and the Uttararāmacarita, at a commentary on a Prakaraṇa, the Mālatīmādhava, at a commentary on a Nāṭikā, the Viddhaśālabhañjikā and so it would be worth our while to have a look at a commentary on another form of Sanrkrit drama that had enjoyed wide popularity, the Prahasana. This will tell us how even the lighter forms of Sanskrit drama were critically studied and commented upon by students of Sanskrit drama and will give also the present study an appearance of an effort to study commentaries on the different forms of Sanskrit drama, the Nāṭaka, the Prakaraṇa, the Nāṭikā and the Prahasana.

The Bhagavadajjukīya of Bodhāyana Kavi is by far the best 'Prahasana' that we possess today. As the internal evidence indicates, it is an early play and possibly belongs to the times of the other celebrated prahasana, the Mattavilāsa. The Bhagavadajjukīya reveals that Buddhism was on the decline and that there was something like a revival of the orthodox Brahmanism. Our play indeed can be regarded as an orthodox one in its teaching and outlook since it reveals an ultimate conversion to established Brahmanism. Whatever its religious outlook may be, its author reveals in no uncertain manner, his wonderful sense of the comic and the satirical. Taking advantage of the ancient beliefs like those of the 'para-kāya-praveśa', entering into the body of another person by yogic prowess, Bodhāyana has given us what can be discribed as a perfect modern farce.

The story is briefly thus : Śāṇḍilya who had formerly been a Buddhist Śramaṇaka, has now taken himself to a new teacher, a Hindu Parivrājaka, the Bhagavān in the play, and the play opens with the teacher and his new student discussing philosophical matters. While the lesson is going on in a garden, in the region nearby appears a blonde courtezan, Vasantasenā along with her two maids expecting the arrival of her lover Rāmilaka. Śāṇḍilya, receiving his lessons in Yoga from his teacher, has his attention distracted by the appearance of the beautiful courtezan and in spite of reprimands from his teacher, is drawn towards the fair girl. To his great dismay, Vasantasenā is bitten by a serpent and falls down unconscious. Śāṇḍilya unable now to restrain himself goes to her with a view to helping her only to find her dead. The deserted Bhagavān, the Parivrājaka thinks this to be a very good opportunity to display his yogic powers to his erring disciple and to win him back, enters the body of the dead courtezan, leaving his own body. As the Bhagavān enters the body of Vasantsenā she regains her consciousness and comes back to life to the delight of all who take their efforts to revive her as successful not knowing the part of the Bhagavān in the affair. To the dismay and surprise of all, the revived Ajjukā, in fact the Parivrājaka in the body of Ajjukā continues the philosophical lesson and all the others unable to follow her take her as having gone mad. In the meanwhile the servants of Yama having realized their mistake in taking away the life of Ajjukā due to mere similarity of name Vasantasenā, bring the soul back to be placed in her body and finding her body as occupied by another soul and also finding the body of Bhagavān as vacant, place the soul in it and depart. The desciple finding his teacher Bhagavān lifeless goes to him, only to find the revived Bhagavān continue the amourous talk of the Ajjukā. Śāṇḍilya is at his wit's end, does not understand as to who is Ajjukā and who is Bhagavān and hence the play Bhagavadajjukīya. Yama's man appears again to help the two souls to take to their respective bodies and thus the comedy ends.

The plot has been constructed skilfully and there is admirable wit and humour as well as satire in the play. The language is clear and simple and one comes across many fine thoughts happily expressed and for sheer striking originality one may refer to the last verse of the play which contains the description of the setting sun and the red sky :

'astam gato hi dinakṛdgaganāntalambī mūṣāmukhastha iva taptasuvarṇarāśiḥ /
yasya prabhābhiranurañjitameghavṛndam ālakṣyate dahanagarbhamivāntarikṣam // 36.

One need not be surprised at the wide popularity of this 'gem of the Prahasanas, prahasanaratnam. The author is Bodhāyana Kavi, certainly not identical wiih Bodhāyana, the celebrated Vṛttikāra of the Vedānta, and it is suggested that this Bodhāyana Kavi came from the South and belonged to the Baudhāyana School.

This pleasant comedy has been commented upon by a pupil of the great Nambudiri scholar Nārāyaṇa Bhaṭṭa of Meppattur who lived about 1590 A.D. His pupil who has chosen to remain anonymous, could therefore be placed at the beginning of the Seventeenth century and it appears, from his own words at the conclusion of this commentary on the Bhagavadajjukīya, that besides this commentary and also before he wrote this commentary he had written one commentary on a play of Bhavabhūti, possibly the Bhāvārthadīpikā on the Uttararāmacarita. Since the author has not given us his name, he has been described here as Nārāyaṇa Bhaṭṭa-śiṣya.

This commentary, the Diṅmātradarśinī, on the Bhagavadajjukīya is here included for our study because of its intrinsic merits and great interest. The commentator has admiration for the poet and his work and like Ghanaśyāma he writes his commentary with the expressed purpose of expounding the hidden meaning of the play. He observes at the outset

'Bodhāyanakaviracite vikhyāte bhagavadajjukābhihite /
abhineye atigabhīre viśadān adhunā karomi gūḍhārthān//
(p. 1)

In what follows he has attempted to offer systematically a philosophical interpretation of the play in addition to the usual explanation of the text as it is before him. He observes that this Prahasana has a two-fold meaning, 'bāhya', the external one and the other 'ābhyantara' the inner one. Of these two meanings, the bāhya or the apparent one refers to and is in keeping with the nature of the play as a Prahasana while the inner meaning possesses deep philosophical significance and is profound, atigabhīra'. About these two meanings and the actual mode how they are given he has to observe as follows :

> 'atra nāṭyasya prahasanarūpatvāt prathamam bāhyatayā hāsyam vastu yojanīyam / idameva hi asya lakṣaṇam yadalīkenaiva purataḥ prahasanena pāramārthikamartham avadhūya kathyate iti' (p. 10).

He appears to regard the 'prahasana' to be a serious play, an allegory having the two meanings, the hilarious and the serious and in such cases the two kinds of meaning are given in a peculiar manner. For neither the śleṣa, nor the dhvani nor the lakṣaṇā operates here, the basic conditions as required being absent altogether here and again the vācyatā does not give the inner meaning readily. This is remarkable discussion revealing as it does his close acquaintance with poetics and a fine grasp of literary criticism. He observes in this context:

> 'prahasanasya iha aprākaraṇikatvāt ubhayaprādhānyabhāvena śleṣaviṣayatāsambhavāt mukhyārthabādhādyabhāvena lakṣaṇāyāḥ api anupapatteḥ puraḥsphūrtyā ca śabdaśaktimūladhvanerapi viṣayīkartum aśakyatvāt bāhyatvam iti / tadvadeva itarasya arthasya paścātpratīteḥ nigūḍhatayā avasthānāt ca vācyatāvyākopād ābhyantaratvam ityapi vaktumeva yuktam ityavaseyam' /(p. 10).

Having made his views thus clear he proceeds almost everywhere to give the bāhya and the ābhyantara meaning and make it clear. He explains the inner idea of the play in the following words 'atra idam anusandheyam:

> 'asmin nāṭyarase nisargagahane yogīndraśiṣyāvubhau
> ātmānau parajīvaśabdakathitau anyā tathaivājjukā/
> mūlādhārasamudgatā sasuṣirā nāḍī suṣumṇā' pare
> ceṭyau cobhayapārśvage sasuṣire nāḍyāviḍā-piṅgale //
> avidyā gaṇikāmatā mahān rāmilako mataḥ /
> vidya vikalpasaṅkalpau kālastu yamapūruṣaḥ //
> evam prekṣāmayaṁ yogaṁ yuñjan nārtakatāpasaḥ //
> pratyañcam acyutam sadyaḥ sākṣātkṛtya sukhī bhavet
> iti // (p. 55)

Thus the Bhagavat and Śāṇḍilya, his pupil are the Lord and the Soul. The Gaṇikā Vasantasenā is the Suṣumṇā vein and the two ceṭīs by her sides are the veins Iḍā and the Piṅgalā. The mother of the Gaṇikā is avidyā and Rāmilaka is the Mahān; the Vidyā represents the oscillating human thoughts, the Vikalpa and the Saṅkalpa and finally the Yamapūruṣa is the Kāla. It is very difficult to say whether our commentator is giving us his original ideas or following an earlier way of interpretation of this play, a possibility which is indicated by the words 'iti' at the end.

With these ideas firmly set in his mind, he proceeds to explain the entire play accordingly. For almost every sentence and expression he has to offer a bāhya meaning and the ābhyantara meaning. In the process, he has explained certain ideas in a very interesting manner. Thus the 'bhikṣā' for which the teacher and the pupil set out, is really the understanding of the nature of Brahman, 'brahmasvarūpagrahaṇam'. (p. 26) Again the word 'kārṣāpaṇa' has its bāhya meaning, money, dhanalava, and its ābhyantara meaning regard and attachment, mamatva. (p. 61). In the very opening verse itself we have the word 'rāvaṇa' explained to us as 'rāvayati duḥkhayati jantūn iti rāvaṇaḥ saṁsāraḥ' this miserable life that causes anguish to the creatures and 'rudra' is 'saṁsaraṇaduḥkhena rodanāt rudraḥ, śāṇḍilyaḥ'. (pp. 2-3). The 'ekakālabhaktatva, of the Baudhas is taken as referring to their 'kśaṇabhaṅgavāda, the doctrine of momentariness. (p. 13). The Buddhist view that 'āhāra-pramāda' is 'sarvapramāda' has obviously the glutton's sanction but it has its deeper meaning also since 'āhāra' means mokṣa, salvation, 'āhriyate sampadyate iti āhāraḥ moksaḥ'. (p. 49). Sentences in the dialogue also have come in for a similar treatment and one may refer to the following to illustrate the point :

When the beautiful Gaṇikā Vasantsenā dies of the serpent-bite, Śāṇḍilya is all upset and finding the Bhagavān Parivrājaka unmoved, almost abuses him : 'ā apehi, akaruṇa, niḥsneha, karkaśahṛdaya, duṣṭabuddha, bhinnacāritra, kūraśakaṭa, mudhāmuṇḍa'. (p. 70-71). The bāhya meaning here is obvious and it refers to the indifference and apparent callousness of the Bhagavān in the face of the sad calamity that has befallen the fair girl. This is also an outburst of a young lad perhaps interested in the lady and the words therefore are to be understood against this background. The commentator explains the bāhya-artha in keeping with this context but adds that the ābhyantara-artha is a praise of the Parivrājaka since the desciple has a great regard for his teacher. He proceeds to explain thus :

> 'anyastu bahumatyatiśayenastutireva / akaruṇa..guṇātītasya tava mamatā nāstyeva/niḥsneha, snehaḥ sarvānarthakara iti śravaṇāt snehādhīnatā'pi nāstīti bhāvaḥ / karkaśahṛdaya, hṛdayaprakṣobharahita ityarthaḥ / bhinnacāritra, yatyāśṛtakriyābhimānarahita / kūraśakaṭa, kūram annam tṛptikāritāsādharmyāt atra brahma ucyate / sākṣātkṛtabrahmasvarūposi iti yāvat / mudhāmuṇḍa, brahmalokaprāptyartham hi turīyāśramavihitācārānuvartanam jīvanmuktasya bhagavatā tadapekṣā nāstyeva iti bhāvaḥ, /(pp. 70-71).

To take another instance : The Parivrājaka has asked Sāṇḍilya to lead the way to the garden and while about to enter, Śaṇḍilya seeing something on the tree and scared, ohserves :

> 'paurāṇikyāḥ mama mātuḥ śrutam aśokapallavāntaraniruddhaḥ vyāghraḥ prativasati/tataḥ bhagavāneva purataḥ praviśatu, aham pṛṣṭhataḥ praviśāmi'/(p. 34).

The 'bāhya artha' is too obvious to need any explanation but having explained it as it should be, the commentator explains the 'ābhyantara' meaning thus :

> 'ābhyantarastu-paurāṇikyāḥ niṣṭhāyāḥ mātuḥ codanāyāḥ / paurāṇikyā ityanena kartṛguṇanirapekṣatayā prāmāṇyasya svatastvam pratipāditam/māturiti viśvasanīyatādisādharmyāt codanāyāmadhyavasāyaḥ / śrutam avadhāritam / indriyahāritasādharmyāt aśokapallavaśabdena viṣayāḥ kathyante / niruddha ityanena duravabodhatā kathitā / hiṁsratvasādharmyāt ca viśayābhisaṅge vyāghraḥ ityadhyavasāyaḥ /tasya ca hiṁsratvam bhagavadgītāyām uktam 'dhyāyato viṣayān..buddhināśāt praṇaśyati' iti / ratyuddīpanabhūte asmin ārāme praveśāt mama viṣayābhisaṅgo niyataḥ bhavet / paścātpraveśe tu jīvanmuktasya

bhagavataḥ prabhāvāt utpattikṣaṇe eva vinaśyet iti bhāvaḥ' / (pp. 34-35).

What was really a peacock has been taken to be a tiger by Śāṇḍilya and when the Parivrājaka makes him realize his mistake, he observes : that the tiger has fled away assuming the form of a peacock, 'aviha, dasīe vutto vaggho morarūvam gahṇia palāadi' and this is interpreted by the commentator as 'atra vyāghro mayūrarūpam gṛhītvā ityanena hiṁsrarūpaḥ viṣayābhiṣaṅgaḥ cittopaśamānukūlaḥ jātaḥ iti kathyate / palāyate ityanena tādṛśarūpaḥ api krameṇa vilayam ca gacchati iti' /. For a similar effort on the part of the commentator, a reference could be made to his comments on the very first speech of Śāṇḍilya where he gives us an account of himself. (pp. 8-14).

This is really evidence enough to indicate the ingenuity of the commentator, in giving us the 'bāhya and the ābhyantara' meaning everywhere in a play which is a 'prahasana'. This effort to interpret a Prahasana as a serious play must be put down as a unique one and does deserve our admiration. The commentator here reminds one of Pūrṇasarasvatī who also reads philosophy in the Mālatīmādhavam of Bhavabhūti Has this trend anything to do with the traditional devotional Kerala mind ? One wonders.

The author of the Diṅmātradarśinī is a well-read scholar and he quotes from the Bhāgavata (p. 39), the Bhagavadgītā (p. 35) and gives us occasionally 'smṛtivacanas'. (p. 17, 26). He has given us a new reading in 'akleśāt madhu vindeta kimartham parvatam vrajet' (p. 19) for the line 'arke cet madhu vindeta' etc. We have 'atke and abke' for 'arke' but here we get 'akleśāt' which deserves to be noted. Gauḍapāda has given us this verse in his commentary on the Sāṅkhyakārikās. He does not discuss the alaṅkāras and only occasionally notes dramaturgic details like 'saṅgīta' (p. 4) āmukha (p. 6). As a matter of fact the words of the Sūtradhāra that 'atha tu nāṭakaprakaraṇodbhavāsu vārehāmṛgaḍima-samavakāravyāyogabhāṇasallāpavīthyutsṇṣṭikāṅkaprahasanādiṣu daśajātiṣu nāṭyaraseṣu hāsyameva pradhānamiti paśyāmi' (p. 4-5) have given rise to a controversy regarding the interrelation of the ten forms but our commentator has no comments to offer here.

One may entertain legitimate doubts as to how far this farce can bear the weight of this serious philosophical meaning that has been read into it by the commentator. That this Prahasana of Bodhāyana was regarded as a serious play is indicated by a verse that occurs in one of its manuscripts and which runs as

> 'bodhāyanakaviracitam bodhāyatanam vimuktiśāstrāṇām/
> prahasana-ratnam pratnam bhavatu mude bhagavadajjukīyam vaḥ //(p. 99)

Our commentator also appears to refer to some earlier interpretation along these lines when he quotes some verses to explain the central idea of the play. (p.55), a fact to which a reference has already been made. Further, the commentator is seen observing in his concluding verse of the commentary, after telling us that he has already written a commentary on the work of Bhavabhūti, that he is now writing a commentary on the work of Bodhāyana :

> 'teneyam viṣametivṛttagahane baudhāyanīye punaḥ /
> nāṭye garbhitaśāstrajṛmbhitavacogambhīragumbhe kṛtā //
> (p. 99).

The Diṅmātradarśinī, therefore, reads like an essay that seeks to interpret a Prahasana as a serious philosophical play. A student of Sanskrit drama should naturally be interested to see this valuable concept of 'laughter having some serious underlying purpose' appearing both in drama and dramatic criticism. This may indicate that after all, the Prahasanas were not frivolous plays, products of mirth and low taste as is generally believed. When the commentator rounds off his commentary in the following words

'iti prahasanābhikhye pūrṇā nāṭyanibandhane /
hāsyagūhitatattvārthe ṭīkā diṅmātradarśinī // (p. 99)

the reader is likely to nod in assent and compliment him for his fine effort in the art of interpretation and for having brought the new concept of 'hāsya-gūhita-tattvārtha' in Sanskrit criticism.

VII. THE ABHIJNĀÑAŚĀKUNTALACARCĀ

(A commentary on the Abhijñānaśākuntala of Kālidāsa)

The Abhijñānaśākuntalacarcā is a commentary on the Abhijñānaśākuntala of Kālidāsa by a writer who remains unknown to us and in all probability hails from Kerala. It is a remarkable effort and compels our attention because of the valuable help it offers for a better understanding and appreciation of the play. It would be worth our while to have a look into it, for not only will it introduce us to a masterly commentary on the great play, but it will enable us to compare it with the Arthadyotanikā of Rāghavabhaṭṭa and thus to have a comparative study of two commentaries on one and the same play. The author does follow the usual pattern of the commentaries of explaining the text and the difficult words in it, of offering grammatical explanations and of attempting an analysis of the plot and of the rasa-scheme, but what deserves our attention is his discussion of the problems to which other commentators do not appear to have paid any attention whatsoever. The very name Abhijñānaśākuntalacarcā is significant and one regrets the fact that the work is not before us in a complete form since we have the discussion of the author only upto a portion of the sixth act. His Carcā of the latter part of the sixth act and of the whole of the seventh act is not before us. The author, though unknown, could safely be placed after Pūrṇasarasvatī whom he quotes and imitates. Pūrṇasarasvatī is usually placed towards the end of the fourteenth century and our author followed him. Since the manuscripts of this work are available only in the Malayalam script and since the author shows intimacy with the plays of Bhāsa, it could be surmised that he came from the South and perhaps from Kerala. It would be hazardous to try to be more definite than this regarding his time and personality. His is a pleasing personality for he appears to have had in him something of a Rāghavabhaṭṭa, something of a Ghanaśyāma and also something of a Pūrnasarasvatī, for he has a delicate sense of fine appreciation which Rāghavabhaṭṭa possesed, he quotes profusely and from many authors just as Ghanaśyāma does and like Pūrṇasarasvatī he writes in a very charming style.

The author is a very well-read person and he always elucidates and substantiates his discussions by freely referring to other plays, poems, works on dramaturgy and poetics and to authorities. In the process he has given ample evidence of his critical and judicious reading and of his tendency to compare and to evaluate. Among the works and authorities referred to, we find Anargharāghava (p.4,5), Avimāraka (28), Āścaryacūḍāmaṇi (20, 28) Uttararāmacarita (47), Karpūramañjarī (12), Kalyāṇasaugandhikam (13), Cārudattam (12, 21, 22, 23), Dūtaghaṭotkaca (13, 24), Nāgānanda (3, 28) Pañcarātra (13), Prabodhacandrodaya (4, 23), Bālacarita (28), Bālarāmāyaṇa (7, 28), Bhagavadajjukam (13), Mālatīmādhava-vyākhāna (5), Mālavikāgnimitra (2,3, 28), Ratnāvali (17), Vikramorvaśīya (2, 3), Vīṇāvāsavadatta (2,26), Svapnavāsavadatta (20, 28). This list is an impressive one and reveals how the author has tried to carry out a critical examination of the Śākuntala by freely referring to the known excellent dramatic compositions. For dramaturgic discussions he refers to Daṇḍin (81), Daśarūpa (4, 55), Dhanika (52, 181), Dhvanikṛt (12, 47, 101), Nāṭakābharaṇa (4), Nāṭyaśāstra (5), Bahurūpaka (2, 70), Bharata (151), Bharatasaṅgraha (54), Bhāvaprakāśa (78), Bhojarāja (54, 132), Mahimabhaṭṭa (82, 86). Vāmana (83, 100), Vyaktiviveka (132), Śṛṅgāraprakāśa (70) Sāhityasāra (18, 19, 27). While offering his explanations of the text before him, he has not neglected to note the views of other commentators of the Śākuntala and he refers to one Tippaṇakāra (31, 33, 73, 77, 88, 93) and to Kṛṣṇācārya (79), both of whom, from the references to them, appear to have been commentators of the Śākuntala. Amongst the poetical compositions referred to, we find the Kumārasaṁbhava (75, 132), Bhartṛhari (93), Mahābhārata (34, 56, 61, 83, 108, 121, 137), Meghasandeśa (87), Raghuvaṁśa (79, 114, 118, 126, 133, 139, 149); but so far as lexicons are concerned only three or four are referred to and these are the Amarasiṁha or Siṁha (13, 14, 32, 38, 53, 66, 72, 74, 80, 82, 97, 99,

107, 129, 145, 155, 164, 168, 171, 172, 176, 179), Keśava (32, 69, 84, 109), Yādava (33, 35, 43, 80, 156) and Halāyudha (91, 163). This fact can be considered as significant since it indicates that the approach and treatment of the commentator is predominantly literary. For once, we have here a commentator who studies, compares and appreciates and discusses problems of different types technical, literary and aesthetic.

A reference could be made to his dramaturgic discussions in this context. Commenting on the text 'nāndyante tataḥ praviśati sūtradhāraḥ' he notices that the text is placed, as is seen from the different plays both before and after the first verse. This, according to him, raises the problem whether the first verse is to be regarded as a nāndī or not. In an effort to study this problem of nāndī, he has gone to the Anargharāghava, Vīracarita, Mālatīmādhava, Veṇīsaṁhāra, Vīṇāvāsavadatta, Bālarāmāyaṇa, Mālavikāgnimitra, Prabodhacandrodaya and has also referred to the views of Bahurūpa, Pūrṇasarasvatī and of the Nāṭyaśāstra. He has pointed out the contradiction in the views of Pūrṇasarasvatī and one regards the entire discussion of the nāndī as a scholarly essay on the Nāndī in Sanskrit plays. (2-8). He has ably shown that all the Vṛttis are present in the Śākuntala. (48). He observes that it should not be held that since we do not have much of song and dance in the play, the Kaiśikī is absent here since the Kaiśikī is associated with song and dance, 'bahunṛttagītā'. After all, he rightly points out, song and dance are the 'upalakṣaṇa' of 'śṛṅgāra-ceṣṭā' and we have a good deal of such activity both on the part of the hero and the heroine in this play. The Sāttvatī is present primarily in the actions of the hero that reveal his excellent qualities, his valour, śaurya, is seen in the 'iṣṭivighnaśamana' in his removing the danger to the sacrifices of the sages in the hermitage of Kaṇva; his sense of justice is seen in the manner he disposes off the case of the drowned merchant, 'nauvipannasārthavāhadhane dharmasthitiḥ'; his courage is seen when his memory is clouded on account of the curse, 'śāpavismṛtau dhairya' and his humility is seen in the homage paid by him to Mārīca, 'mārīcādyupasthāne vinayaḥ'. He observes that it should not be argued that since we do not have any of the aṅgas of the Sāttvatī, like the sallāpaka, the utthāpaka, the saṅghātya or the parivartaka, here the vṛtti is absent, for when the aṅgas are absent it follows that the aṅgī is also absent. Here the vṛtti is seen in the actions of the hero, 'iyam nāyakasya vyāpārātmikā', and he gives his verdict that the enumeration of the aṅgas is only formal, 'aṅgasaṁkhyā tu aupacārikā'. (49). The Ārabhaṭī is to be seen in the curse of Durvāsas and in the action of Mātali when he beats the Vidūṣaka to arouse the anger and valour of the hero. The Bhāratī Vṛtti being 'vāgātmikā' as a matter of fact pervades the entire work, 'sarvatra vartate'. Our commentator's discussion of the Avasthās, the Arthaprakṛtis, the Sandhis and the Sandhyaṅgas is not as complete and rigorous as that of Rāghavabhaṭṭa; for we find only the Ārambha among the Avasthāpañcaka pointed out (44) and so also only the Bīja (44) and the Bindu (68) from the Arthaprakṛtis have been shown. Of the five Sandhis, only the Mukha Sandhi has been discussed and from amongst its twelve aṅgas, only the Upakṣepa (44), Parikara (50), Vilobhana (59), Paribhāvanā (63), Bheda (64) Samādhāna (65) and Karaṇa (69) have been located. In his commentary on the later portions of the play, he has not said anything about these aspects of the play though there cannot be any doubt about his close familiarity with the dramaturgic theory as can be seen from his discussions about the Vīthyaṅgas and the like (16) and the Sandhis and the Sandhyaṅgas (70). He echoes the views of the dramaturgic writers when he observes that it is not necessary to use all the aṅgas enumerated, in a play. Some of the aṅgas may be dropped, for a play does not suffer in its excellence even if a few of them are dropped : 'tathā ca abhiyuktatama-kālidāsādi-prabandheṣu prameyānusāreṇa tricaturādyaṅgavilope'pi śobhāprakarṣo dṛśyate eva'. (70). Having pointed out a few of the aṅgas, he prefers to leave it to the readers to find out the others for themselves and puts forth the plea that he is following this course, for otherwise the bulk of the work would increase. In humility, he pleads ignorance as well. 'evam anyāni ca sandhisandhyaṅgādīni sahṛdayaiḥ svayameva paryālocanīyāni / granthagauravabhayāt ajñātatvāt ca tatra na vicāryate iti śivam'. (70).

What is of greater interest to us is the fact that our commentator is seen differing from Rāghavabhaṭṭa in the placement of the aṅgas : thus Rāghavabhaṭṭa places the Upakṣepa, the first aṅga of the Mukhasaṅdhi, at the very outset where the Vaikhānasa pronounces the blessing on the King in 'janma yasya purorvaṁśe etc.' and the King decides to see the daughter of Kaṇva even after knowing that Kaṇva is absent, for this is bīja-nyāsa according to him, 'janma yasya ityādinā tām drakṣyāmi ityantena mukhasandheḥ upakṣepa iti prathamam aṅgam upakṣiptam' (p.16). This author, however, places it much later, at the place where the king expresses his desire for Śakuntalā in 'yadāryam asyām abhilāṣi me manaḥ'. (44). He is seen arguing that the Ārambha cannot be placed any earlier, as for instance, in 'idam kilāvyājamanoharam vapuḥ' or in 'sarasijamanuviddham' or in 'adharaḥ kisalayarāgaḥ' etc. for at all these places we have only the love at first sight, mere attraction, 'nayana-prīti-mātrabhāvāt. It would appear that Rāghavabhaṭṭa thinks that the decision of the king to see Śakuntalā in the āśrama was frought with consequences and the blessing from the Vaikhānasa was a prophecy to be fulfilled. Our author, however, seems to regard the play as a story of romance and so places the Ārambha in the abhilāṣa of the king. We find a similar difference in the placing of the Sandhyaṅga Karaṇa, which according to Rāghavabhaṭṭa is to be seen where Priyaṁvadā does not allow Śakuntalā to leave reminding her of her debt of 'two turns' and where the king desires to redeem Śakuntalā by giving the ring, for this is the 'prakṛtārtha-āraṁbha' ; but our author places it in the king's 'gacchati puraḥ śarīram' etc. at the end of the act, which is the beginning of the separation, vipralaṁbha-ārambhaṇa. (69) This difference as well as the one to be seen in the placement of the other aṅgas as well, throws good light on the views of these two authors regarding the analysis of the plot-construction of the play. Our author tries to indicate the interrelation between the incidents in the play, as for instance, when he observes (p. 36) that the throbbing of the arm of the King is an indication of the blessing about to materialize, 'anena pūrvaprastutāyāḥ āśiṣaḥ phalaunmukhyam āsāditam'. Rāghavabhaṭṭa has in his comments tried to indicate the rise and progress of the emotion of love in the minds of the lovers, through all the states, daśās, but here have been shown only a few of these daśās like the abhilāṣa, cintā or the nidrāccheda. One may hence feel with justification that Rāghavabhaṭṭa is not only more copious but is also more systematic as well as penetrating in his appreciation and criticism than our author is.

Yet there are some points where our author is in a way more helpful and original in his comments than Rāghavabhaṭṭa. He discusses the very title of the play (15-16) in a very illuminating manner, a discussion in which Rāghavabhaṭṭa apparently is not interested. The title Abhijñāna-śākuntalam offends against the grammatical rule 'adhikṛtya kṛte granthe', since this rule requires the vṛddhi of the first vowel and not of the 'a' in the second word ; the correct form therefore would be Ābhijñānaśakuntalam. According to this very rule, the title could also be Śākuntala. Abhijñānaśākuntala also would be permissible, if the dvandva were to be treated as a unitary aggregate according to the observation 'sarvo dvandvo vibhāṣayā ekavad bhavati', then Abhijñānaśākuntalam also would be correct. He observes, 'abhijñānam ca śakuntalā ca.. tathāpi syāt. (16)

But prehaps of greater interest is his discussion regarding the presentation of the heroine to the hero as is to be found in Kālidāsa's first act. The play is no doubt based on the story in the Mahābhārata but this source narrates the meeting of the two in quite a different manner, there being no reference to the friends of Śakuntalā or to the watering of the trees and the like. Our author raises the problem in this manner : 'nanu atra itivṛttam itihāsa-prasiddham ityuktam, itihāse tu naiva nāyikādarśanam pratīyate' (44). He gives the Mahābhārata account and compares it with that of the poet and points out that there are many additions made by the poet. The temptation to quote the entire discussion cannot be resisted, because of its importance. He observes :

'itihāse tu naiva nāyikādarśanam pratīyate..na punaḥ āśrama-bāla-mahīruhasecanasamaye avalokanam abhihitam, na ca asyāḥ sakhīsadbhāvaḥ uktaḥ / api ca mṛgayāprasaṅgamātreṇa āśramaprāptirakathi, na āśramamṛgānudhāvanena/ na ca tadantare vaikhānasopasthānam tenāśrama-nivedanādikam vā praṇītam / nāpi kaṇvamuniḥ śakuntalāyāḥ pratikūla-daivaśamanāya somatīrtham gatavān, śakuntalayaivānyathā niveditatvāt / tat kathamatra vastu prakhyātam bhavet/ upariṣṭādapyanasūyayā rājñe śakuntalotpattinivedanam itihāsaviruddham / tathā rājānveṣi-paurajanāgamāt sambhramaḥ, vidūṣakaprasaṅgaḥ, senāpatyādivyavahāraḥ, ṛṣiprārthanayā rākṣasanivāraṇārtham āśramanivāsaḥ,durvāsasaḥ śāpānugrahau ca svakapolakalpita eva, na bhūtārthaḥ / garbhiṇyāḥ satyaḥ sakuntalāyāḥ bhartṛsamīpaprāpaṇam atīva-itihāsaviruddham, yata āśrama eva putram suṣuve śakuntalā/..tatkatham garbhiṇyā eva nagaraprāptiḥ/ tatra sārṅgaravagautamīprabhṛtibhiḥ saha rājñaḥ vivādopi na vāstavaḥ, ṛsīṇām nagarapraveśakathanāt / gautamīkathaiva nāsti /...punarasyāḥ apsarobhih mārīcāśramaprāpaṇam, dhīvarādaṅgulīyakaprāptiḥ, tadā śāpanivarttanam, rājñaḥ paścāttāpādikam, indrānurodhāt asuravadhārtham mātalinā saha svargamanam, pratyāgamane mārīcāśramāsādanam, tatra śakuntalāputradarśanādikam ca sarvam etat vitatham itihāsa-adarśanāt / kintu parikalpitameva / evam sthite kathamatra vastu prakhyātameva bhavitum arhati, miśrameva nūnam bhavitum arhati' / (46).

He then points out that history and drama are two different things and a dramatist has to carry out a very judicious selection, omission and additions to the original account furnished by history so as to suit his purpose. He observes :

'atra ucyate-iha khalu kevalam prakhyātenaiva vastunā kiñcinnāṭakam-upanibadhum na pāryate / tatra hi nāyakasya rasasya vā viruddha anupayogino vā kathāṁśāḥ sambhavanti/ na ca bhavantyupayoginaḥ / taiḥ tathā ca nāṭake na bhavitavyam, tasya rasaikaparāyaṇatvāt / ataḥ tatra tādṛśānām aṁśānām parityāgo anyathākalpanam vā parikalpanam vā saṁvidhīyate / na caitāvatā tasya prakhyātatvam hīyate' / (46).

One feels that one is reading Clayton Hamilton's 'So you are writing a Play'. In the drama, the rasa is the main thing and in good plays there is always a skilful blend (miśra) of the prakhyāta and the parikalpita or the utprekṣya and the proportion of these two elements may differ from play to play as in the cases of the Vīracarita and the Uttararāmacarita. (47).

The author then proceeds to analyse the first act and justify the poet in the following manner :

'nāyakadarśanakalpanāyām kim nimittam/ rasādivirodhaparihāro nimittam / yathāprasiddhadarśane hi sahāyābhāvāt kanyā svayameva svagatavacanam saparyām sambhāṣaṇam ca kuryāt / tatra dhārṣṭyāt nāyakālokanādau veśyābhāvaśca tasyāḥ prasajyate / tad rasasya pratikūlam nāyikāyāśca nocitam/ atra svayaṁvacanaparihārāya sakhīkalpanam / tatsāhityenoṭajāṅkaṇādau devatārcanasnānādikāle padasparśanādāśramadharmabhūtavṛkṣasecanasamaye darśanam bahumukham sādhīya ityevametat saṁvihitam/ āśramapraveśaucityasampādanārtham āśramamṛgavadhanivartanārtham ca vaikhānasopasthānam/ tatra śakuntalādaivaprātikūlyenābhisaṁhitam sadṛśapratilābhavilambanam śamayitum kaṇvaḥ somatīrtham gata iti vacanam tattapaḥ-prabhāveṇa nṛpaterevāśramaprāptyādyabhiratim sūcayitum/ tacca nāyakasya lokottaramaudāryam prakāśayitum / .....vidūṣakādīnām nāṭyanyāyāt /...svato nāyakasya nāyikāvismaraṇe rasabhaṅga iti durvāsaśśāpanirmāṇam, tathā sati rasādeḥ na kathaṁcit kśatiḥ / punaranugraheṇāṅgulīyakādarśanāt smaraṇaviṣādavilāpādibhiḥ prema pariposayan svātantryam ca nodricyate iti kṛtvā vismaraṇādyaṁśaparityāgaḥ /.. jyotiśa apsarobhiḥ hemakūṭākhyakimpuruṣaparvatapradeśaprāpaṇaṁ tasyā mahābhāgyādiguṇaprakaṭanārtham / tatprāptyupāyatayā nāyakasya daiteyavadhāya indrānurodhāt prāptāt svargāt pratyagamanavelāyāṁ mārīcāśramāvataraṇaṁ viracitam / evam avaśiṣṭakalpanāyāmapi upapattiḥ ālakṣyatām /' (47).

It is to be remembered that a Sanskrit commentator is writing these lines. Who can deny him the credit of having studied the play very critically, remembering very well the abiding principles of art and literature. Rightly does he point out that considerations of art, rasa and propriety made Kālidāsa introduce all these elements in his plot.

This very critical attitude of the commentator is to be seen in his effort to point out the interrelation between the different incidents as well as the expressions in the play. Thus he tells us that in the third act in the direction 'mukhamasyāḥ samunnamitum icchati, śakuntalā nāṭyena pariharati' Kālidāsa is contemplating of the later separation, vipralambha, and also of the poignant 'muhuraṅgulisamvṛtādharoṣṭham'. The keen disappointment of the hero in this immortal 'unkissed kiss' has been very well brought out by the commentator in his 'pānāya upakrāntasya tadalābho duḥkhāt duḥkhatara iti bhāvaḥ'. (122). He is quick to notice that the verse 'sāyantane savanakarmaṇi sampravṛtte' etc. with which the act closes is the poet's clever device for effecting a transition in the mood of the hero : nāyakasya rasāntarapraveśam āha'. (125). His comment on the celebrated curse of Durvāsas is that it is tit for tat, 'yādṛśaḥ aparādhaḥ tādṛśaḥ śāpaḥ iti bhāvaḥ / anena śāpena pañcamāṅkasya bījanyāsaḥ kṛtaḥ iti mantavyam'. (127). He tells us that the verse 'antarhite śaśini' with its 'candra-vṛttānta', has an immediate application to and therefore elucidates the main plot and its present state of development, 'prakṛtam artham viśadīkaroti'. (129). With his poetic spirit, he too points out like Rāghavabhaṭṭa that in the exquisite 'bhramara iva vibhāte kundam antastuṣāram' the 'tuṣāra' is 'śāpasthānīya', for we find Rāghavabhaṭṭa here remarking, 'himasya ācchādakatvāt śāpasthānīyatvāt tyāgabhāvaḥ'. (128). While commenting on the two beautiful utterances of Kaṇva : dhūmoparuddhadṛṣṭeriva yajamānasya pāvaka eva āhutiḥ patitā, and 'vatse, suśiṣyaparidattā iva vidyā aśocanīyāsi me saṁvṛttā' he observes, 'tātabhūtena mayā khalu aviditamevānurūpabhartṛlābho ghaṭitaḥ iti prathamenopamānena uktam / vatse iti sambodhanena tasya tadviṣayasya snehasyātiprakarṣatvam uktam / upamānadvayena nāyakayoḥ parasparānurūpyam jagadārādhanīyatvam ubhayalokābhyudayahetutvam sarvapuruṣārthahetutvam askhalitapraṇayavṛttitvam ca ityūdyāsaṅkhyam yvaṅgyam unneyam'. (132) Rāghavabhaṭṭa sees in these expressions, 'kṛtakṛtyatā' of Kaṇva himself in 'pāvake āhutiḥ patitā', anena svasya kṛtakṛtyatā dhvanitā, and of Śakuntalā in the other 'vidyeva aśocanīyāsi saṁvṛttā, anena tasyāḥ kṛtakṛtyatā dhvanitā.' (94).

In his discussions regarding the alaṅkāras and the suggestions or dhvani, this author may not be found to be as learned and as copious as Rāghavabhaṭṭa every time is seen to be, but it is to be admitted that on occasions, he has something very illuminating to offer, something that would do credit even to Rāghavabhaṭṭa. He points out that in the verse 'kṛṣṇasāre dadaccakṣuḥ' etc., Kālidāsa has deliberately used the word 'pinākin' and not the better known ones like 'maheśvara' or 'kapardin'. According to him, the reference here is to the story of Śiva chasing Viriñci who was following his own daughter with amorous intentions. The verse is rendered beautiful by the 'prasāda guṇa' and the 'utprekṣā' alaṅkāra. He thinks the alaṅkāra could be taken as 'viśeṣa' as well and we have the 'upamā' also suggested. He observes, 'atra prasādo guṇaḥ, utprekṣā alaṅkāraḥ, aśakyavastvantarakaraṇātmā viśeṣo vā, upamā vyajyate'. (30). Rāghavabhaṭṭa finds here an allusion to the story of Śiva chasing the sacrifice of Dakṣa that was running having assumed the form of a deer, 'mṛgarūpadharayajñānusāriṇam'. Rāghavabhaṭṭa further observes that the alaṅkāra here cannot be 'Upamā' since the word 'sākṣāt' has been used and the word 'iva' has been placed after the word 'paśyāmi' which indicates action. The idea here appears to be : 'while I am casting my eye on the antelope and on you, I perceive you to be the Pinākin, as it were; thus two actions are indicated here and this fact is of significance. In the Upamā, if that figure were to be read here, we have to take the words as 'sākṣāt paśyāmi' and then the words 'dadaccakṣu' lose all significance. He also thinks that the alaṅkāra Viśeṣa is present here since the one and the same eye is described as being simultaneously present at different places: 'cakāreṇa tulyakālatā dyotyate / tataśca ekasya cakṣuṣaḥ yugapadanekatra vartamānatvāt viśeṣālaṅkāraḥ'. (10). The two commentators seem to be in agreement though they take the mythological allusion differently and so far as poetics is concerned, the two are complementary. Our commentator is alert to comment on the first appearance of Śakuntalā and her two friends in the first act: tataḥ praviśati yathokta-vyāpārā saha sakhībhyām śakuntalā : that is as a matter of fact, highly auspicious and is a clever suggestive device of the poet. He remarks, 'atra munikanyakānām pūrṇakumbhasahāyatayā abhimukhāgamanam prathamadarśane mahattaram mangalam iti boddhavyam, (37) a point about which Rāghavabhaṭṭa has to say nothing. On the beautiful 'navakusumayauvanā vanajyotsnā snigdhapallavatayopabhogakṣamaḥ sahakāraḥ', Rāghavabhaṭṭa suggestively comments 'tattveneti nāyakavyavahārāropāt samāsoktiḥ (23) but our commentator has to add 'anena pādapamithuna-samayojanena asyāḥ manasi yauvanārambhavaśāt anurāgapraveśaḥ sūcyate / yathā murārināṭake pāñcālikā-mithuna-saṁyojanena sītāyāḥ'. Thus he has explained the idea and also has drawn our attention to a drama where a similar device has been used. Like Rāghavabhaṭṭa, our author is also seen analysing for us the clever blend of emotions reflected in Kālidāsa's verses and one may refer to his comments on Duṣyanta's 'vācam na miśrayati yadyapi madvacobhiḥ' etc. Rāghavabhaṭṭa explains the verse and observes 'anena mugdhāyāḥ nāyikāyāḥ gātrajaḥ vilāsa iti bhāvaḥ uktaḥ', but our author adds 'atra lajjā-autsukyayoḥ sandhiḥ'. (6) Like Rāghavabhaṭṭa, he too points out the development of a rasa or of an emotion in a verse and one may refer to his comments on Duṣyanta's 'idam aśiśiraiḥ antastāpāt vivarṇamaṇīkṛtam' etc. where he has pointed out the 'uddīpana-vibhāvas, the anubhāvas, vyabhicāri-bhāvas and also the vipralambha that is ultimately manifested. It is noticed that here Rāghavābhaṭṭa prefers to proceed further without adding anything to his explanation.

The commentator like the actor really adds ten words to the author's one when the former explains and the latter delivers the text. One can in this context refer to the explanation offered by our commentator of 'kiñcid vihasya', a direction by the playwright to Priyaṁvadā, in 'āryasya vacanena anṛṇā idānīm eṣā/(kiñcid vihasya) halā, śakuntale, mocitāsi anukampinā āryeṇā / athavā mahārajena / gaccha idānīm '/. Priyaṁvadā is very cleverly naughty and mischievous in her remarks here and the laughter assigned to her by the playwright is intended to show that she has as a matter of fact understood fully well what has been going on. We find our commentator, therefore, remarking, 'kiñcid vihasya iti / nāyakasya nāyikāyām sphuṭābhiniveśadarśanāt / halā ityādi / ayam tvayi gāḍhābhilāṣaḥ saṁvṛttaḥ, ayam prakāro bahudhāsmābhiḥ parīkṣitaḥ, niścitam ca ayam rājā duṣyantaśca iti / tasmāt prahṛṣṭamanā gaccha ityarthaḥ (65). It should be noted that Rāghavabhaṭṭa is not inclined even to comment on this sentence.

There can be little doubt about the fact that our author has in him the potentialities of Rāghavabhaṭṭa, for this is clear to us from his poetical explanations, happy expressions, clever suggestions and from his appreciation of fine situations. One can refer to his comments on Duṣyanta's 'muhuraṅgulisaṁvṛtādharoṣṭham..kathamapi unnamitam na cumbitam tu' in the third act. Rāghavabhaṭṭa explains this verse and like Ānandavardhana, brings out the 'paścāttāpa' reflected in that significant 'tu' so cleverly placed at the end of the line by the poet. But it is really our author who does full justice to this fine verse. He goes on:

> 'muhuriti punaḥ punaḥ/aṅguli-saṁvaraṇa-paunaḥpunyena tanniṣedhapaunaḥpunyam gamyate / saṁvṛtādharoṣṭham na tu saṁvṛtoṣṭham iti / anena pipāsārthameva nāyakasya cumbanecchā iti dyotyate / uktam ca-adharasya pipāsata mayā te sadayaṁ sundari gṛhyate 'dharoṣṭhaḥ' iti pratiṣedhākṣara iti / anena nāyikāyā aṅgulisaṁvaraṇaniṣedha-nivartanapragalbhatvam dyotyate / mā mā iti pratiṣedhākṣaraiḥ, na tu pratiṣedhavākyaiḥ / anena lajjābhayasambhramādayaḥ vyajyante / aṁsavivarti-iti-anena pratiṣedhākṣareṣvapi nāyakasya anādaraḥ pratīyate / kathamapyunnamitamityanena aṁsavivartanaprayāsasya duḥsādhatvam unnamananirodhapaunaḥpunyam ca dyotyate/ tu-śabdena aṅgulisaṁvaraṇaniṣedhādyanekaprayatnasannidhāpitasya sambhogasarvasvabhūtasya cumbanasya alābhāt viṣādātiśayo dhvanyate / sa ca vipralambham paripuṣṇāti / pakṣmalākṣyā ityanena akṣisaundaryakatha-

nena tatkālollasitā vividhāḥ bhāvāḥ vyajyante/tathāhi cirābhilaṣitasya sambhogasya acintitopanatatvāt harṣaḥ, tathaiva tadvighnitatvāt viṣādaḥ, samāgamasyedamprathamatayā lajjātrāsau ca / evamupayogino'nye bhāvā draṣṭavyāḥ / sarve bhāvāḥ cakṣuṣi vyajyante iti nyāyāt / atra nāyikāgatalajjā nāyakagatamautsukyam ca utkaṭatvena pratīyate /aṅgulisaṁvaraṇādayo lajjayā anubhāvāḥ, saṁvaraṇaniṣedhādayaśca autsukyasya / etau parasparam aṅgulispardhāsāmrājyamanubhavataḥ/cumbitam taditi pāṭhāntaram /(124).

This is indeed a very creditable exposition and even Rāghavabhaṭṭa could not have done better. Of course, the pāṭhāntara noted, 'cumbitam tat' is to be discarded on the authority of the text itself and of Ānandavardhana also.

But the most remarkable feature of this commentary that distinguishes it from all the rest of the commentaries whether on this play or on any other, is the awareness it reveals of the fact that this is a play to be performed on the stage, an awareness which is reflected in many of its discussions. The commentator discusses the presentation of the first scene on the stage, where Duṣyanta is chasing the deer in a chariot. It is difficult to imagine that a real chariot was introduced on the stage. The commentator observes, (30)

'atra ratho na raṅge praviśyate, api tarhi tasya sūcanameva kriyayā yuktam na tvavataraṇam kāryam, turaṅga-(mṛ) gapotarathavimānānām teṣām ākṛticihnaiḥ vidhānamuktam gativicāre iti/gativicāre coktam-gajavājirathādīṁstu cihnamātreṇa kārayet/vāhanārthaprayogeṣu raṅgāvataraṇeṣu ca //iti/athavā tṛṇavastrādiracito rathaḥ praveśayitavyaḥ / taduktam vastrakṛtānyathavā rathagajavājivimānayānāni / kartavyāni vividhaiḥ tathā ca vividhapraharaṇān // iti /(30)

Further, he raises the interesting question that when in actuality, neither the chariot, nor the horses nor the king are moving, then how could it be said that 'dūram amunā sāraṅgeṇa vayam ākṛṣṭāḥ'? He is seen observing :

'nanu atra rathena drāghīyān mārgo laṅghyate ityucyate,

tanna yuktam, aṅkaviṣayatvāt, aṅke dūrādhvānam niṣiddham / yadāhurdūrādhvānam vadham ityādi/ucyate-nātra rājā sūtaśca rathe sthitau padacaram kurutaḥ, rathaśca na calati, tasyākṛticihna-viṣayatvāt vastukṛtatvādvā / na khalu sākṣādratho raṅge avatāryate ityuktam, ato gamanameva nāsti/tat kuto dūrādhvagamaḥ/tarhi kathamamī dhāvantīdyādi kathyate / kathanamātram tat nāṭyanyāyāt/ratho vegena gacchati, turagā dhāvanti, dīrgho' dhvā laṅghitaḥ ityādi tannigadyate eva tathābhāvena na tu kriyate/kriyatecet raṅgam vimucya dhāvanena pradeśāntare avasthānamāpatet/kathanamātre na kaścid doṣaḥ/ evamupariṣṭāt svargādārabhya hemakūṭagatamārīcyāśramaparyantam rathenāvataraṇe /...tatra raṅge sarve deśāḥ /'(33).

What we have is a mere description and not actual movement. The stage is wide enough to include all the three worlds. Such a view of the stage gives the much needed Shakespearean freedom to the actors and the playwright, for by merely lowering a board with a title or with a descriptive sentence, the scene could be placed in a forest or in a castle or on an island or on the waves of an ocean. No other commentator seems to have taken any notice of these problems connected with a play and its prayoga, production on the stage.

Our author has discussed the problem of the production of the play, has also said something about the plot and its construction by the poet, and he has said something significant about originality in literature. Pointing out the similarity between 'śakyam aravindasurabhi' etc. of Kālidāsa with 'śakyam añjalibhiḥ pātum vātāḥ ketakagandhinaḥ' of Vālmīki he observes :

'atra purātanakavidṛṣṭārthasvīkāro na doṣāya, dhvaniprabhedānugṛhītatvāt / taduktam dhvanikṛtā—

ato hyanyatamenāpi prakāreṇa vibhūṣitā

vāṇī navatvamāyāti pūrvārthānvayavatyapi // iti / atra pavanasvabhāvavarṇanam vipralambhāṅgatayā camatkāraikaghanatvāt sahṛdayahṛdayamullāsayati / tatra tu prāvṛdvarṇanamātraparameva' /(101).

When all these aspects of this commentary are taken into consideration, its value becomes clear. The author has a style of his own and he writes in a simple yet elegant manner and at many places he reveals influence of Pūrṇasarasvatī, as for instance in phrases like 'nāyikā-prativacana-mahotsava-pramuditaḥ nāyakaḥ (106), hṛdayasannihite dayite śilādipratimāyām paradevatāvat satatasannihite (117), lajjābhārabharitahṛdayā (120) and so on.

The Abhijñānaśākuntalacarcā, judged by all standards, must be reckoned as a remarkable piece in dramatic criticism in Sanskrit. The author, though anonymous, need not fear comparison with any one, Ghanaśyāma or Pūrṇasarasvatī and even when compared with Rāghavabhaṭṭa, his great qualities do not allow his lustre to fade. There can be no two opinions about the value of his effort to enable us to appreciate this great play of Kālidāsa which he describes as 'rasanirbhara, (70), śṛṅgārarasasarvasva (96), prasannagambhīra (125), rasaniṣyandi (170). A remarkable and fine performance indeed !

VIII EPILOGUE

This short survey of a few select commentaries might indicate in some measure the importance as well as the worth of such commentary literature. The general belief that these commentaries are not worth much, are at the best word for word paraphrases and in themselves do not represent in any way any deliberate and conscious effort to judge a work of art, here in this case the dramas, on aesthetic principles, is indeed as mistaken as it could be. It is no use trying to judge these commentators like Rāghavabhaṭṭa, Pūrṇasarasvatī, Vīrarāghava, Jagaddhara, Ghanaśyāma, Sundarī and Kamalā, Dhuṇḍhirāja and others, by applying them the yard-stick fashioned after a perusal of critical literature now available from the West. For, like Literature, Criticism also has its own tradition. This fact has got to be remembered when these commentators are subjected to a critical examination and a judgement is passed on them.

This does not mean that these commentators need any defence for the effort they have put in to enable us to understand and appreciate the master-pieces in Sanskrit dramatic literature. The relevant question in this context is whether they do or do not assist us materially in properly understanding and appreciating the works on which they choose to comment. The foregoing study clearly indicates that the reply to such a question will have to be positively affirmative and indeed, this fact in itself is ample justification for a serious study of these commentaries.

These commentators have taken care to equip themselves properly for their self-chosen task, for almost each one of them is a critical student of logic, grammar, poetics, dramaturgy and is also conversant with many other complimentary branches of knowledge. This is a fact that is clear to one who tries to understand the literary background of these commentators as revealed in their commentaries through the numerous quotations that they give. Their knowledge of the different lexicons is admirable as is their familiarity with the classical literature. Their comments reveal their insight into literary criticism and also their capacity to think for themselves. Further, the fact that they often are seen criticising even the recognised masters should prove that they were not blind in their praise and wilful in their criticisms. Their respect for the author did not rob them of their judgement and this rare quality of theirs deserves to be admired.

As has been already shown in the foregoing study, the contribution of these commentators to a proper appreciation of a play is immense, being varied. They have pointed out the dramatic and dramaturgic technique when they refer to the types of the hero and the heroine or to the Avasthās and the Arthaprakṛtis or to the different Sandhis and the Sandhyaṅgas. They have also discussed the questions of Rasa and the Alaṅkāras, for they have tried to indicate the emotions developed as well as the figures of speech employed. They have revealed their close acquaintance with poeties by entering into discussions regarding the Dhvani, the Alaṅkāra and the like. They have also noted the variant readings for the text they are studying and offered interpretations of the texts before them as well as of the variant readings which they note. Thus their help for the understanding of the text is also really considerable. They have given their interpretations and while doing this have also taken note of other interpretations offered by others and have subjected these other interpretations to an examination. Metre and Grammar also have been properly attended to. They have tried to point out similar thoughts to be met with elsewhere to the one they are explaining and have tried to understand imitations and influences. It would therefore be no exaggeration to say that they have practically done everything that a critic is expected to do. Further, their contribution to history of Sanskrit literature also is significant since through their citations and references they throw valuable light on Sanskrit works and authors.

These commentators have a place all their own in Sanskrit literary criticism. The nature and value of their contribution can be clear only when the help they offer is compared with the help offered by writers on poetics or on dramaturgy. One might for the sake of elucidation take the case of Rāghavabhaṭṭa whose Arthadyotanikā on the Abhijñānaśākuntala of Kālidāsa we have studied in the foregoing pages.

Ānandavardhana in his epoch- making work, the Dhvanyāloka, recognises the greatness of Kālidāsa whom he describes as a 'mahākavi'. Observing that a peculiar charm always graces the works of great poets and it reveals their genius, he goes on to say that after all there are only a few poets, hardly two or five, that belong to this class of Kālidāsa. He observes 'yena ativicitrakaviparamparāvāhinī saṁsāre kālidāsaprabhṛtayo dvitrā pañcaṣā eva va mahākavaya iti gaṇyante'. (p. 31). Again while discussing the necessity of admitting the descriptions of 'inanimate' in poetry and their relation to the Dhvani, Alaṅkāra and the like he quotes from the Vikramorvaśīya of Kālidāsa to illustrate his point and prefaces the citation with the remarks that if such descriptions are not admitted then great poetical compositions, the treasurehouses of Rasa as it were, would have to be declared as being void of Rasa: 'atha satyāmapi tasyām yatra acetanānām vākyārthībhāvaḥ nāsau rasavadalaṅkārasya viṣayaḥ ityucyate, tanmahataḥ kāvyaprabandhasya rasanidhānabhūtasya nīrasatvam abhihitam syāt' (p. 92). Even though the remark appears to be of a general nature, it is to be remembered that it introduces a verse from Kālidāsa. Ānandavardhana himself, it appears, was strongly influenced by Kālidāsā as would be indicated by his words 'ādikaveḥ... krauñca-dvandva-viyogotthaḥ śokaḥ ślokatvamāgataḥ' in Kārikā V in the First Uddyota. Again, even when his innate high sense of propriety and delicacy makes him adversely criticize poets who indulge in the description of 'sambhoga-śṛṅgāra' of gods and their wives, he is cautious while speaking of Kālidāsa and his description of 'sambhoga' of Śiva and Pārvatī in the Kumārasambhava, Canto VIII. He does remark that it is like describing the love of parents and so highly indecent 'sutarām asabhyam' (p. 192) but adds earlier that the genius of the poet, however, makes it acceptable: 'tathā hi mahākavināmapi uttama-devatā-viṣaya-prasiddha-sambhoga-śṛṅgāranibandhanādyanaucityam śaktitiraskṛtatvāt grāmyatvena na pratibhāsate/yathā kumārasambhave devīsambhogavarṇanam' (p.176). Ānandavardhana has referred to and quoted from Kālidāsa on several occasions (pp.92, 93, 109. 132, 133, 255, 202, 203, 204, 206. 222, 260, 295, 328. 342, 352, 301), from his poetical works and the plays and from the Abhijñānaśākuntala with a view to showing the great poetic skill and rich aesthetic sense of Kālidāsa in the use of the various elements of poetic embellishments. Thus, we are told that in 'calāpāṅgām dṛṣṭim' the alaṅkāra 'svabhāvokti' has been used to harmonise well with the rasa : 'atra hi bhramarasvabhāvoktiralaṅkāro rasānuguṇaḥ' (p.109-110). We are also told that in 'kimiva hi madhurāṇām maṇḍanam nākṛtīnām' the word 'madhurāṇām' is a suggestive one—vyañjakatvābhiprāyeṇaiva kṛta—(p.155). Again, in the verse 'muhuraṅgulisaṁvṛtādharoṣṭham' we have the words 'kathamapi unnamitam na cumbitam tu' where the 'nipāta tu' is vyañjaka, 'atra tu śabdaḥ'(p. 204) since it conveys the sense of repentance for not having 'kissed' and the sense of near fulfilment in having 'raised' the lovely face. In the line 'prasnigdhāḥ kvacidiṅgudīphalabhidaḥ sūcyanta evopalāḥ' in the celebrated verse 'nīvārāḥ śūkagarbha etc'., the upasarga 'pra' in 'prasnigdha' is suggestive, vyañjaka, since it conveys the 'sarasatā' of the iṅgudī-phala and through it the sylvan wealth of the āśrama. (p. 204). But more than these observations that undoubtedly reveal a superb critical insight, this great rasika does not help us to appreciate the excellence of the Śākuntala. One may say with ample justification that it was not his aim. But then, this fact would reveal the importance of the help offered by Rāghavabhaṭṭa. He seems to have taken his cue from Ānandavardhana and Dhanañjaya, when towards the end of his commentary he gives a rasa-analysis of the play and comments favourably on the handling of the story by Kālidāsa. He remarks : 'nāyikā bālam gṛhītvā svayam tadgṛhagamane dhṛṣṭatayā anaucityam/kulāṅganāyāḥ gāndharva-vivāhaḥ svayam niṣpādyaḥ/tasya mahā-puruṣasya karaṇam vinā sammohaḥ so'pi anucita eva iti anena kavinā kaṇvena tapasvibhiḥ saha prasthāpanam śāpopyanākarajopi nibaddhaḥ'/Rāghavabhaṭṭa closes his commentary with a brilliant analysis of the play and with some very significant remarks revealing Kālidāsa's greatness and while doing so, has referred to Ānandavardhana three times and to Dhanañjaya once and therefore he could be given the due credit of having examined the play in the light of the views of these authorities.

Mammaṭa too, like Ānandavardhana, does not offer us much help so as to render Rāghavabhaṭṭa superfluous or commonplace. He refers to the verse 'gāhantām mahiṣāḥ etc.', for pointing out the 'kāraka-prakramabhaṅga' in the line 'visrabdhaiḥ kriyatām varāhapatibhiḥ mustākṣatiḥ palvale' and he suggests its correction as 'visrabdhāḥ racayantu sūkaravarāḥ mustākṣatim palvale' praising this latter as flawless, aduṣṭa. (p.374). The verse 'grīvābhaṅgābhirāmam is cited to illustrate the 'bhayānaka rasa'. (p.109). Mammaṭa refers to the other works of Kālidāsa to elucidate his points and to illustrate the alaṅkāras as well as the doṣas, the figures of speech and the defects. Thus to illustrate 'kriyayoḥ samuccayaḥ' he refers to 'ayamekapade etc. (p.690), to 'are rāmāhasta (Vik) as suffering from the flaw of 'anuvādayukta (404), to 'asyāḥ sargavidhau' as an illustration of 'bheda-anukta-sasandeha' (p.591) ; 'to kātaryam kevalā nītiḥ (Rv.) as suffering from the flaw of redundancy of words (p.307) ; to 'krodham prabho saṁhara' (Ks) to illustrate the krodha in a divya character (p.443) ; to 'kva sūryavaṁśaprabhavaḥ' (Rv) as an illustration of the alaṅkāra Nidarśanā (p.614) ; to 'kvākāryam śaśalakṣmaṇā' (Vik) as an instance of Bhāvaśabalatā (p. 126) and of a happy inter-relation between the 'bādhya-viruddha-sañcāri' and the 'prākṛta-rasa' (p.447) ; to 'gṛhiṇī sacivaḥ etc.' as a case of the Viśeṣa alaṅkāra (p.743) ; to 'candram gatā etc. (Ks) to illustrate 'khyāte arthe nirhetoḥ aduṣṭa' (p.411). It might be regarded as significant that most of these citations are to be found in the seventh Ullāsa where Mammaṭa discusses the defects in poetry, the kāvyadoṣas. Mammaṭa does not, as is to be seen from his remarks, approve of the description of the Saṁbhogaśṛṅgāra between Śiva and Pārvatī in the Kumārasaṁbhava. Judging on the whole, it would appear that to Mammaṭa, Kālidāsa was not as great as Ānandavardhana saw him to be. This is the impression that the

Kāvyaprakāśa creates on one and hence it becomes all the more significant when we find Rāghavabhaṭṭa speaking with the accents of Ānandavardhana.

One might turn to a yet later and equally discerning critic who had also the true poetic instinct in him, the illustrious Jagannātha Paṇḍita. To Jagannātha, Kālidāsa was a 'mahākavi (p.172) and he compliments him for his 'amum purā paśyasi devadārum' for after this we get, 'iti prāyuṅkta mahākaviḥ'. He refers to Kālidāsa on four or five occassions, (pp.200, 215, 259, 301 and 501) and all these references are to be found in the course of his discussions of rasa, figures of speech and the like. Jagannātha refers to the 'rati' between Duṣyanta and Śakuntalā (pp.23 27) and bases his discussion of our experience of a rasa by referring to our experience in this matter. This discussion is no doubt interesting since it involves the actor, naṭa, the spectator, the sāmājika, rati, Duṣyanta and Śakuntalā. But all this has a purely academic flavour and the discussion does not have any bearing on the excellence of the play itself, the work of Kālidāsa. Thus Jagannātha too does not make Rāghavabhaṭṭa superfluous.

Nor is Pūrṇasarasvatī or Ghanaśyāma superfluous, for with Bhavabhūti perhaps the case is much worse in as much as these theorists have very little to say about him and his plays, the Mālatīmādhava fairing a little better at their hands than the Uttararāmacarita. In the Dhvanyāloka, Ānandavardhana has not much to say about Bhavabhūti and it may be regarded as significant that there is not a single quotation from him, though Ānandavardhana quotes from Kālidāsa, Māgha, Bhartṛhari, Harṣa, Bhaṭṭa Nārāyaṇa and from works like the Mahābhārata, the Rāmāyaṇa, the Gāthāsaptaśatī, the Gauḍavaho, the Harivijaya, the Gītā and the Sārṅgadharapaddhati. Even in the context of Karuṇarasa he prefers to refer to the Rāmāyaṇa. Even when he has the 'Rāma' context, he refers to 'rāmo' smi sarvam sahe' (p.71) and to 'rāmeṇa priyajīvitena tu kṛtam premṇaḥ priye nocitam' but to nothing from the Uttararāmacarita. Ānandavardhana discusses the art of constructing a good plot and has to offer really valuable advice to authors in the matter of introducing changes in a celebrated and familiar story, 'kathāmārge na ca alpo'pi atikramaḥ,' ; in the matter of introducing new elements conducive to the development of the rasa, 'svatantratayā rasānuguṇam kathāntaram utpādayet' ; about the use of the Sandhis and the Sandhyaṅgas as contributory to the rasa 'sandhīnām tadaṅgānām ca ghaṭanam rasābhivyaktyapekśayā' ; about the skilful delineation of the rasa by maintaining its continuity as well as variety, 'uddīpanapraśamanam anusandhiśca' ; about the employment of the alaṅkāras with a view to contributing to the development of the rasa, since writers often go after the alaṅkāras and ignore the rasa,' 'alaṅkāra-nibandhanaikarasa, anapekṣitarasa' ; and such other matters which need very careful attention of the author. While discussing these matters he has referred to Kālidāsa, Sarvasena, Harṣa and himself. One is tempted to think that at least in the discussion of the style to be resorted to for the delineation of the Karuṇarasa, there could have been some occasion to refer to the poet whom tradition regards as the only one poet capable of successfully developing and delineating this rasa—'kāruṇyam bhavabhūtireva tanute'. We find Ānandavardhana remarking that for the development of the karuṇa and the vipralambhaśṛṅgāra, style full of compounds should not be resorted to, 'karuṇa-vipralambhayoḥ tu asamāsaiva saṅghaṭanā' (p.179)...tayorhi sukumārataratvāt svalpāyāmapi asvacchaṭāyām śabdārthayoḥ pratītiḥ mantharībhāvāti... prasādātikrame hi asamāsāpi saṁghaṭanā karuṇavipralambhaśṛṅgārau na vyanakti' (p.180)..nāṭakādāvapyasamāsaiva saṁghaṭanā' (p.187). In his entire discussion, it is significant that Ānandavardhana felt like referring to a verse from the Veṇīsaṁhāra of Bhaṭṭa Nārāyaṇa, the celebrated 'yo yaḥ śastram bibharti', etc. One is obviously not justified in drawing conclusions from non-mention and silence, but one must confess that this passing over of Bhavabhūti by a great critic like Ānandavardhana does strike one as significant. Was indeed Ghanaśyāma when criticising Bhavabhūti for his 'mugdhaḥ praṇāmāñjaliḥ' and 'sphurati me garbhabhāraḥ' taking his cue from Ānandavardhana who remarks that 'ratiḥ hi bhāratavarṣocitenaiva vyavahāreṇa divyānāmapi varṇanīyā iti sthitiḥ' (p.191) or are we to say that Ghanaśyāma was simply being overfastidious ?

In Mammaṭa we have a better notice of Bhavabhūti taken, since we get about nineteen quotations from him, but it is to be noted that of these nineteen quotations not even one hails from the Uttararāmacarita, the distribution of the quotations being eight from the Mahāvīracarita and eleven from the Mālatīmādhava. Most of these references are in the context of the discussions of rasa and the sañcāris, the bhāvasandhi, the kramabhaṅga and the different alaṅkāras as well as of the kāvyadoṣas, the defects in poetry. (pp,96, 103, 110, 125, 180, 181, 294, 310, 314, 374, 356, 382, 329, 398, 414, 424, 466, 679). The Mālatīmādhava has been more fortunate in being referred to by other writers like Bhoja and others also. But it cannot be said that these discussions severally or put together, at any time, throw significant light on Bhavabhūti's art and poetry and on that count we are in a better position to understand him.

In the Rasagaṅgādhara, Jagannātha Paṇḍita refers to the verse from Bhavabhūti, 'purā yatra srotaḥ etc', only to dismiss the view expressed in the Kuvalayānanda that in this verse we have a 'sārūpyāt samāsokti' (p.382-383). It is true that Jagannātha deliberately composed his own verses to illustrate his points, but he is also seen referring to verses of other poets and one is struck with the fact that when he quotes verses in the context of Rāma, to illustrate his 'dainya' (p.80-81), his soliloquy or 'vitarka' about Sītā after her abandonment (p.91), his self-condemnation after the act of abandonment (p.176), not even once does he quote from or refer to the Uttararāmacarita. It is to be conceded that it would be unreasonable to expect a writer to quote from a particular work, yet the fact remains, for whatever it is worth, that Jagannātha does not go to Bhavabhūti when he, one may feel, supplies verses which could be, if not better, at least as good as the verses with which he has sought to illustrate his points. Thus it would appear that Pūrṇasarasvatī, Vīrarāghava and Ghanaśyāma have a place all their own in literary criticism.

The Daśarūpa of Dhanañjaya is a regular work on

dramaturgy and this work does refer to these two masterpieces, the Abhijñānaśākuntala and the Uttararāmacarita to illustrate a few points. But its partiality for the Ratnāvalī and the Veṇīsaṁhāra is too obvious to escape notice, a partiality that is to be seen in later works on dramaturgy also, works like the Nāṭyadarpaṇa or the Nāṭakalakṣaṇaratnakośa. In the Daśarūpa, from the Śākuntala are illustrated the 'Pātrasūcana' in 'tavāsmig ītarāgeṇa' (p.145) ; Prayogātiśaya in 'eṣa rājeva duṣyantaḥ (148) ; Śobhā in 'anāghrātam puṣpam' (121) ; Mādhurya in 'sarasijamanuviddham (122) ; Mārdava in 'medacchedakṛśodaram' (157); and Abhilāṣa in 'asaṁśayam kṣatra-parigrahakṣamā', (260), From the Uttararāmacarita, we have the Drava illustrated in 'vṛddhaste na vicāraṇīyacaritāḥ' (47); Śakti in 'virodhaḥ viśrāntaḥ' (48); Avalagita in the Sītā-tyāga (150) ; Vākkeli in 'tvam jīvitam' (152); Gaṇḍa in 'ayi deva upasthitaḥ' (153); Adhvaśrama in 'alasa-lulita' (186) Moha in 'viniścetum śakyaḥ' (199) ; Deśavibhāva in 'smarasi sutanu tasmin parvate' (253); Prāṇayamana in 'asminneva latāgṛhe' (263); Sambhoga in 'kimapi kimapi mandam' (271); Vilāsa and Dhairya in 'dṛṣṭistṛṇīkṛta' (93) and the 'anukūla ekanāyikā, in Rāma's 'advaitam sukha' etc. (88). We find a few illustrations hailing from the Mahāvīracarita and the Mālatīmādhava and occasionally from the Mālavikāgnimitra and the Vikramorvaśīya. The other later works on dramaturgy more or less follow the lead of the Daśarūpa in this matter. It would be an interesting study if all these observations to be met with in the works on rhetorics and dramaturgy on a particular play are brought together and are compared with the study of the play as available in a commentary on the said play by some commentator. The nature of the commentary as 'applied criticism' and also its intrinsic value would be clear from such a study. It will be evident that the commentators have an importance all their own. That their criticism is not purely subjective should be clear from the authorities whom they quote, on whom they rely and whom they appear to follow. Mātṛgupta, Bharata, Ānandavardhana, Vāmana, Dhanañjaya, Udbhaṭa are the names to be met with in these commentaries and the definitions of the alaṅkāras hail from various standard works on poetics. The commentators hence are in the literary tradition of writers on dramaturgy and poetics and not outside it.

The commentaries are indeed complementary to works on dramaturgy and poetics, though it is true that these commentators do not attempt a critical survey of all that has been said elsewhere whether about a play or about a verse. Thus no commentator points out that in 'advaitam sukhaduḥkhayoḥ etc.' we have Rāma as an 'anukūla' nāyaka being 'ekanāyikā' (DR. p. 88); that we have here 'preyaḥ' which is 'priyatarākhyānam as well as 'sthairya' as Bhoja points out (SP. 508,520). One feels that if all that has been said about the Mālatīmādhava is brought together, it would be clear perhaps how Bhavabhūti wrote the play with the thought of the critical literature of the Alaṅkāraśāstra in his mind. All this material as well as the commentaries help us to appreciate the play better and give us an idea of the views of the earlier generations of critics about it. The commentaries therefore deserve to be read as supplementary to whatever we get in the works on dramaturgy and poetics.

A comparative study of many commentaries on one and the same work or play also often proves very interesting. It is seen that the personality of the commentator plays a decisive role in the performance and the approach. How could one afford to forget Rāghavabhaṭṭa, Pūrṇasarasvatī and Ghanaśyāma ? One has to go through the commentary of Ḍhunḍhirāja on the Mudrārākṣasa to see how rigorously a commentator tries to explain and understand a classic. The Prāṇapratiṣṭhā of haughty Ghanaśyāma and the Camatkāra-taraṅgiṇī of Sundarī and Kamalā, the learned ladies make a very interesting reading side by side and the commentaries proclaim their writers.

This study is intended to be an argument for a more intensive study of the commentary literature so far as dramas are concerned. There is to be seen growing a deplorable tendency of utterly neglecting these commentaries and of decrying them, perhaps even without reading them. One may refer in this context to many of the modern editions of the Sanskrit plays where usually two sins are committed. They drop the Prakrit speeches altogether and give instead the Sanskrit 'chāyā' and secondly they do not give any commentary that could offer material aid for the correct reading and understanding of the text.

Of these two sins, the first one of dropping the Prakrit text is to put it mildly an 'offence'. Dramaturgic texts specifically lay down that characters in a play—excepting some and that too with good reasons—use the different Prakrits and it is clear that this was an attempt at realism. Śakuntalā and Sītā, Mālatī and Vasantasenā, these fairies of the Sanskrit dramatic woodlands open their mouths to drop 'Prakrit pearls'. It is only when occasion demands that Sanskrit is resorted to and the dramatists are careful to introduce such speeches with the direction 'sanskṛtam āśritya'. How without the Prakrits is one to understand the clever and beautiful puns in the Mṛcchakaṭika of Śūdraka? For instance, there is no reason why Śakāra should understand Vasantasenā's 'sāntam' as 'śrāntam', for neither was he short of hearing nor she of indistinct speech. It is the original Prakrit form that is of significance here, capable as it is, of giving rise to both these forms. It is thus against the very spirit of Sanskrit dramaturgy and drama as well, to ignore the Prakrits.

Secondly, every effort should be made to give the commentaries their proper place. It is no exaggeration to say that one has yet to come across any exposition of the Abhijñānaśākuntala that would make the reading of the Arthadyotanikā redundant. The reading of the commentaries does not only help the reader in his appreciation and understanding of the text but it often opens up fresh grounds for him for investigation. It is not only going through a commentary or merely reading more Sanskrit or having some help for the understanding of the text, but it is also having a fund of rich and varied information, of different readings, interpretations, works and authors perhaps hitherto unknown. The importance of the dramaturgic texts like the Daśarūpa, the Nāṭyadarpaṇa, the Bhāvaprakāśikā, the Nāṭakalakṣaṇaratnakośa and also the commentaries cannot be any time overstated. It is the Nāṭyadarpaṇa that tells us of the lost 'Devī-candragupta' and it is the Bhāvaprakāśikā which tells us of a fuller 'Svapnavāsavadatta' of Bhāsa. It is Ghanaśyāma, Sundarī and Kamalā who tell us that Kālidāsa was Īśvarakṛṣṇa Bhartṛmīḍha. It is obvious that every commentator is not a Rāghavabhaṭṭa or a Ghanaśyāma. But then there is no greater injustice than condemning without reading and also than being condemned without even a perusal. There is a debt of gratitude that we owe to these commentators and this debt deserves to be acknowledged without any reservation whatsoever.

The tradition of Sanskrit commentators is indeed glorious. The best of minds have devoted themselves to the task of commenting on earlier texts, but this did in no way deter them from showing to us the quality of their mind and their independent thought as well as approach. Such commentaries of outstanding merits were raised to the status of the Bhāṣyas and these became standard works for later ages. This is an ancient time-honoured vocation graced by Śaṅkarācārya, Abhinavaguptācārya and Sāyaṇācārya. Commentaries in other branches of Sanskrit learning have received due attention of a student of Sanskrit both ancient and modern. Commentary literature on the dramas, the pañcamahākāvyas, poems like the Gāthāsaptaśatī and the like and on the works on dramaturgy and poetics is considerable and this too needs due attention. It is both a pleasure and a privilege to read a Sanskrit classic in the company of a Mallinātha or a Rāghavabhaṭṭa or a Pūrṇasarasvatī or a Ghanaśyāma who enlighten us as well as provoke us. I would therefore like to close the present discussion by paying these commentators my homage with the celebrated

"tattvam kimapi kāvyānām jānāti viralo bhuvi /
mārmikaḥ ko marandānām antareṇa madhu-vratam //"

APPENDIX

Manuscripts of commentaries

Plays	*commentaries*
Anargharāghava	Bhavanātha Miśra, mentioned in Bomb. ed.
	Dhaneśvara Radh. 23. Lahore 6.
	Dharmānanda DC. XXI 8355
	Harihara, Tanj. VIII 3315. Rice. 262.
	Jinaharṣagaṇi PR IV 25.
	Kṛṣṇa, DC., XXI. 8357. Tanj. VIII
	Lakṣmaṇasūri, Ed. Madras.
	Lakṣmīdhara, Rāmānandāśrama, DC XXI 8359. Tanj. VIII 3319.
	Mānavikrama TC. II 2580.
	Naṛacandra, CC. SKC. 77. Kh. 64. 65.
	Puruṣottama, CC. 1. 15.
	Pūrṇasarasvatī, TC. III, 3880.
	Rucipatidatta Ed. Bomb.
	Śrīnidhi CC. 1. 15.
	Tripurāri, CC. 1. 15. Rice. 262.
	Vikramīya, Oppert 2560.
	Viṣṇu Paṇḍita, DC. XXI. 8360. HZ 331.
	Viṣṇu Bhaṭṭa, DC. XXI. 8381. HZ 331.
	One anonymous
	Oppert gives also : 2960, 4736. 5820. 6132. 6133. 7815. 7816. II 6540.
Abhijñānaśākuntala	Abhirāma CC. 1. 23 II. 187 III. 6
	Bālagovinda, TC. IV. 4340.
	Candraśekhara, Ia. 77a. I.Ō.77. 1398.
	Ḍamaruvallabha, Oppert II. 8384. Mack. 109

D.V. Pant, Ed. Calc.
Dakṣiṇāvartanātha, TC. III 3982.
Ghanaśyāma, Ed. Trivandrum
Kāṭayavema, Ed. Bomb.
Kṛṣṇanātha Pañcānana, Oppert II. 8382.
Nārāyaṇa
Prākṛtācārya
Premacandra, Calc, ed.
Rāghava DC. XXI. 8370. Ed. Bomb.
Rāma Pisharoti, Ed. Trichur
Rāmavarman
Rāmabhadra, L. 2824.
Śaṅkara, Oxf. 135a.
Śrīkṛṣṇanātha,
Śrīnivāsa DC. XXI. 8373.
Veṅkaṭācārya, Ed. Madras.
Vidyāsāgara, Ed. Calc.
Five anonymous DC. XXI. 8373. 8374. TC. III 3480. 3985.

Ayyābhāṇa (*Śṛṅgāratilaka*) — Rāmacandra, Oppert II. 7784. 8385.

Uttararāmacarita — A. Barooah, Ed. Calc.
Abhirāma, TC. III. 2823.
Ātmārāma, TC. III. 1599. 1601.
Bhotājī Śāstrin, Ed. Nāgpur.
B.S. Ghate, Ed. Nagpur.
Ghanaśyāma, TC. III. 1720.
J. Vidyāsāgara
Lakṣmīkumāra Tātācārya,
Lakṣmaṇasūri, Ed. Kumbhakonam
Nārāyaṇabhaṭṭa I. O, 16o5. Oxf. 136a. L. 2479. k. 68.
Pūrṇasarasvatī
Premacandra Tarkavāgīśa, Ed. Calc.
Rāghavācārya, CC. 1. 63
Rāmacandra, Ed. Madras
Tārākumāra Cakravartin, Ed. Calc.

	Vīrarāghava, Ed. Bomb.
	One anonymous TC. III. 3503. 3836. CC, I. 63.
Uṣārāgodaya	Commentary. NW. 618.
(Nāṭikā, Rudra-candra-deva)	
Kaṁsavadha	Padakaumudi BA. 16.
(Nāṭaka, Kṛṣṇa, Śeṣakṛṣṇa)	A Commentary, Burnell, 167 b.
Karpūramañjarī	Anantadāsa, TC. III. 3936.
	Dharmacandra, CC. I. 82. II. 15. III. 18. PR. IV. 25. V. 423.
	Dharmadāsa
	J. Vidyāsāgara, Ed. Calc.
	Kāmarāja, kh. 83.
	Kṛṣṇasūri, DC. XXI. 8355.
	Nṛsiṁharāja, TC. 382.
	Pītāmbara, W. 1559. 1560.
	Vāsudeva, Ed. Bomb. K. 70 Peters. 3. 393.
	A commentary in Radh. 20.
Dāna-keli-kaumudi	Jīva Gosvāmin, L. 3278.
(Bhāṇa, Rūpa Gosvāmin)	Raghunāthadāsa, Keith 268.
	A commentary in Hpr. I. 164.
Ḍamaruka	Candraśekhara, HZ. 3. 1674.
(Ḍamaruka-Ghanaśyāma)	
Dhanañjaya-Vijaya	Rāmakṛṣṇa Sarman, BI. 61. AS. P. 86.
(Vyāyoga, Kāñcanācārya)	
Nāgānanda	Ātmārāma, CC. I. 283.
	N.C. Kaviratna, Ed. Calc.
	Śivarāma, Ed. Trivandrum.
	Śrīnivāsācārya, Trichinopoly
	Oppert also gives 2866.
Prabodhacandrodaya	Ādyānātha, Ed. Shibpur
	Appayya-Dikṣita, Taylor 1,222. Oppert II. 2070.3712.
	Devarāja, Tb. 61 (1-3)
	Gaṇeśa. CC. III. 75. I 0. 591. Oxf. 141 a. Peters. 5. 425.

Ghanaśyāma, Tanj. VIII. 3432.
Govindāmṛta, TC. III. 3318.
Maheśvara Nyāyālaṅkāra, Ed. Calc. Tub. 23.
Rāmadāsa, Trav. 77. BC. 303. BD 503. I 0. 436. 483. 591. 1917 A. 2037. 2359. Ft. 446. Rgb. 378. Stein 78. Oxf. 141 a. k. 70. kh. 76. B. 2. 120. N.P.V. 186. Burnell. 169 b. Poona 224. Oppert II. 7640. Bp. 262. SB. 309
Rudradeva, Ed. Bomb. Oxf. 141 a. L. 2368.
R.V. Dikshita, Ed. Poona.
Sadātmamuni CC. II. 78.211. P. 10.
Subrahmaṇyasudhī, DC. xxi. 8429. Tanj. VIII. 3436.
Oppert also gives : 2898. 6045. 8096. BP. 55.

Prasannarāghava — Lakṣmaṇa, TC. III. 3220.
Lakṣmīdhara, Cg. 2. 204.
Narasiṁha or Rājarāya TC. III. 3394.
Raghunandana, CC. II. 81. 211. IOC., VII. 4158. L. 3306. (Act. I)
Veṅkaṭācārya, Ed. Bomb.
Oppert II. 954. Is also a commentary.

Priyadarśikā — R.V. Kṛṣṇamācārya, Ed. Srirangam

Bālarāmāyaṇa — J. Vidyāsāgara, Ed. Calc.
Lakṣmaṇasūri, Ed. Tanj.
One anonymous—Tanj. VIII 535.

Bhaimīpariṇaya — Oppert I. 3443 commentary.
(*Drama—Rāmaśāstrin*)

Mallikā-Māruta — Ed. Calc. and Mysore
(*Prakaraṇa—Uddaṇḍa*) — with commentary, DC. XXI. B 446.

Mahānāṭaka — 1. Bālabhadra Miśra K. 76. BP. 55. 263. 357.

Candraśekhara Hpr. 2. 157. I0. 237.
Madhusūdana, Calc. ed. DC. XXI. 8449.
Mohanadāsa Ed. Bomb. I. 0. 1279. Peters. 438-9.
Nārāyaṇa, CC. I. 438. II. 100. 216.
R. Śiromaṇi, Ed. Calc.
Vidyāvinoda Bhaṭṭācārya AS. P. 139.

Mahāvīracarita Ātmārāma NW. 620.
Vīrarāghava, DC. XXI. 8451. Madras GOL. 61. 67.
Oppert 2401. 5818. II. 8312. Rice. 260. Ulwar 1014.

Mālatīmādhava Bhāvaprakāśa, BC. 120.
Dharānanda PRV. Bd. 438. Peters. 5. 430.
Jagaddhara, Ed. Bomb. Oxf. 136a. L. 2137. k. 72.
J. Vidyāsāgara, Ed. Calc.
Kuñjavihārī, Ed. Calc.
Mānāṅka, PR. III. 11. 291. I. O. 158. Oxf. 136a.
Nārāyaṇa, B. 2. 122.
Pūrṇasarasvatī, TC. III. 4118.
Prākṛtācārya, CC. 1. 453. II. 104.
Rāghavabhaṭṭa NW. 618.
Tripurāri, Ed. Madras.
Other commentaries : NP. V. 126. Oppert 3456.

Mālavikāgnimitra Kāṭayavema, Ed. Bomb.
Mṛtyuñjaya Nissank, Ed. Madras.
Nīlakaṇṭha, Ed. Bomb.
Parīkṣit Kunjunni Raja
Tarkavācaspati, Ed. Calc.
Śrīkaṇṭha TC. II. 820. 2570.
Vīrarāghava, CC. II. 104. 217. Rice. 260.
Other commentaries : Oppert 1988. 2954. NW 624.

Mudrārākṣasa	Abhirāma CC. I. 461. II. 106. 218. III. 99.
	BC.—80 a
	Ḍhuṇḍhirāja, Ed. Calc. Bomb. L. 3008.K. 72. Burnell 171 a. Oppert II. 5870 6382. 8321.
	Graheśvara, DC. XXI. 8472. CC. III. 99. I.O.827. GOL. Madras 70.
	J. Vidyāsāgara, Ed. Calc.
	Keśava-Upādhyāya
	Maheśvara Peters. 3. 395.
	Prākṛtācārya
	Sarabhabhūpa, Tanj. VIII. 3474.
	Svāmi-Śāstrin, DC. XXI. B. 468.
	T. Tarkavācaspati, DC. XXI. B. 548. Ed. Calc.
	Vaṭeśvara Miśra, CC. II. 160. 218. I. O. 827. Oxf. 144a. L. 2484. k. 72.
	Vaṭeśvara
Mṛcchakaṭika	Dharānanda DC. XXI. B 475.
	Gaṇapati CC. I. 465. K. 74.
	Lallā—Dīkṣita, Ed. Bomb.
	Pṛthvīdhara, Ed. Bomb.
	Rāmamayāśraman, Ed. Calc.
	Śrīnivāsācārya, Ed. Madras
	Vidyāsāgara (Jīvānanda), Ed. Calc.
	Other commentaries : NW. 624. D. 2.
Yatirāja—vijaya (*Nāṭaka—Varadācārya*)	A commentary Oppert 5137.
Ratnāvalī	Bhīmasena CC. I. 492.
	Govinda, Ed. Bomb.
	J. Vidyāsāgara, Ed. Calc.
	K.N. Nyāyapañcānana, Ed. Calc.
	Lakṣmaṇasūri, Ed. Calc.
	Mudgaladeva CC. I. 492.
	Nārāyaṇa-Śāstrin Nigudkar, Ed. Bomb.

	Prākṛtācārya CC. II. 115.
	R.V. Kṛṣṇamācārya, Ed. Madras
	Śiva HR. III. 34. 137.
	S. Roy, Ed. Srirangam
	S.C. Cakravartin, Ed. Dacca.
	V.S. Aiyyar, Ed. Kumbhakonam
Rambhāmañjarī (*Nāṭikā-Nayacandra*)	A commentary Peters. 3. 395.
Rukmiṇī-kalyāṇa (*Nāṭaka-Rājacūḍāmaṇi*)	A commentary Oppert 3472. II. 6001. Ed. Madras DC. XXI. 7448.
Vikramorvaśīya	Abhayacaraṇa
	Kāṭayavema DC. XXI. 8510. GOL. Madras 84. Burnell 172a. Rice 264.
	M.R. Kale, Ed. Bomb.
	Rāmamaya CC. I 569. II. 134. III. 120. NW. 626
	Raṅganātha DC. XXI. 8511. Oxf. 135b. K. 74. Bühler 542. FI 444. GOL. Madras 84. I. O. 699.
	Tārānātha, Ed. Calc.
	Other commentaries Oppert 5828. II. 8350.
Vidagdhamādhava (*Nāṭaka—Rūpagosavāmin*)	commentaries : NW. 624. Ulwar 1024.
Viddhaśālabhañjikā	Ghanaśyāma, HR III 1677 Sundarī and Kamalā (wives of Ghanaśyāma) HR III 1676
	J. Vidyāsāgara, Ed. Calc.
	Nārāyaṇa, Ed. Poona CC. I. 292. Tanj. VIII 3664-8
	Satyavrata, Ed. Calc.
	Vāsudeva TC. III. 8870.
	One anonymous DC. XXI. 8518.
Veṇīsaṁhāra	C.R. Tiwary Ed. Benares
	Ghanaśyāma, HR. III. (1905) XI
	Jagaddhara, Ed. Poona.

	Jag Mohan Tarkālaṅkāra, Ed. Calc.
	Lakṣmaṇasūri, Ed. Madras
	Tarkavācaspati, Ed. Calc.
	Oppert also gives : 8363.
Saṅkalpasūryodaya (*Nāṭaka—Veṅkaṭanātha*)	Nārāyaṇa OML. No. 14609. Taylor 1. 13.
	Rāmānujācārya Oppert II. 6716. Ahobala Bl. 292. Oppert 4207. 5800.
	Anonymous DC. XXI 8546.—49. DC. XX. 7977.
Hāsyārṇava (*Prahasana—Jagadīśvara*)	Mahendranātha Oppert 8432. Ulwar 1030

The auther is indebted to Aufrecht's Catalogus Catalogorum and Schuler, M. Bibliography of Sanskrit Drama, (1906) for this information. The debt is gratefully acknowledged.

BIBLIOGRAPHY

1. The Abhijñānaśākuntalacarcā. Author anonymous. Edited by Dr.K. Raghavan Pillai. University of Kerala Sanskrit Series. Trivandrum. No. 195 Trivandrum, 1961.

2. The Arthadyotanikā of Rāghavabhaṭṭa on the Abhijñānaśākuntala of Kālidāsa. Edition of the play by late M.R. Kale. (Seventh Edition revised by K.M. Shembhavanekar). Gopal Narayan and Co. Bombay, 1934.

3. The Camatkārataraṅgiṇī of Sundarī and Kamalā on the Viddhaśālabhañjikā of Rājaśekhara. Edition of the play by Dr. J.B. Chaudhuri. Calcutta Oriental Series. No. 30. Calcutta, 1943.

4. The Dhvanyāloka of Ānandavardhana. Editor Dr. Nagendra. Jñānamaṇḍala Granthamala No. 97. Varanasi Jñānamaṇḍala Limited. Varanasi, 1962.

5. The Diṅmātradarśinī of a pupil of Nārāyaṇa Bhaṭṭa on the Bhagavadajjukīya of Bodhāyana. Edition of the play by P. Anujan Achan. Published from the office of the Paliyam MSS Library Jayantamangalam, 1925.

6. The Kāvyaprakāśa of Mammaṭa. Bhandarkar Oriental Institute. (Revised by Principal R.D. Karmarkar). Poona, 1965.

7. The Prāṇapratiṣṭhā of Ghanaśyāma, on the Viddhaśālabhañjikā of Rājaśekhara. Published in the Edition by Dr. J.B. Chaudhuri. Calcutta Oriental Series No. 30. Calcutta, 1943.

8. The Rasagaṅgādhara of Jagannātha Paṇḍita. Nirnayasagara Edition. Bombay, 1938.

9. The Rasamañjarī of Pūrṇasarasvatī on the Mālatīmādhava of Bhavabhūti Trivandrum Sanskrit Series No. 170. Trivandrum, 1953. Edition of the play by Mahopadhyaya K.S. Mahadeva Sastri. Trivandrum, 1953.

10. The Sañjīvana of Ghanaśyāma on the Uttararāmacarita of Bhavabhūti. Edition of the play by Dr. MM. P.V. Kane and C.N. Joshi. Motilal Banarasidas. (Fourth Revised Edition). Delhi. 1962.

11. The Śṛngāraprakāśa of Bhoja by Dr. V. Raghavan. Punarvasu. 7 Kṛsnapuram Street. Madras 14. Madras, 1963.

I. INDEX OF AUTHORS

II. INDEX OF WORKS